Smell, Memory, and Literature in the Black Country

Sebastian Groes · R. M. Francis
Editors

Smell, Memory, and Literature in the Black Country

palgrave
macmillan

Editors
Sebastian Groes
University of Wolverhampton
Wolverhampton, UK

R. M. Francis
University of Wolverhampton
Wolverhampton, UK

Foreword by
Will Self
Brunel University London
Uxbridge, UK

ISBN 978-3-030-57211-2   ISBN 978-3-030-57212-9   (eBook)
https://doi.org/10.1007/978-3-030-57212-9

Cover credit: Image courtesy of Black Country Living Museum Trust

This Palgrave Macmillan imprint is published by the registered company Springer Nature Switzerland AG
The registered company address is: Gewerbestrasse 11, 6330 Cham, Switzerland

This book is dedicated to Dr. Paul McDonald: the Bellows to our Hearth

Foreword

It's a great honour to have been asked to write a preface to this superb collection of psychogeographic writing about the Black Country. In it you will find a whole series of diverse ways of engaging—via the medium of literature—in this extraordinary region; one which—I think it fair to say—represents a sort of spatio-temporal synecdoche of the island of Britain itself. For here in the Black Country you find the true heart of England, inasmuch as its embodiment is as much a matter of coal, iron and steel, as it is of field, dell and hedgerow. The early industrialisation of Britain meant that its inhabitants were the first in the world to experience the crucial caesura between what the great urban theorist, Lewis Mumford, dubbed 'the eotechnic', and a new era in which the arrival of mechanised transport systems and modes of production brought profound changes to both the sensuous and perceptual apprehension of place and space.

Psychogeography is a term that has—through its cultural diffusion—attained an unfortunately dubious status, oscillating between being an overused buzzword and a piece of recondite jargon. The original Situationist practitioners, being Marxists—and revolutionaries, to boot—understood the *dérive*, or aimless stroll (their principal psychogeographic technique), as simultaneously undermining a society that had commoditised place and space to the point where any individual's journey was predicated on an internalised metric of time and money, and also proposing a new kind of human environment—one allowing for the playful, the sensuous and the subjective.

In Britain, those attracted to psychogeography—who seldom embrace the revolutionary programme of their French cousins—have often been branded as self-indulgent types, whose urban exploring is merely a pretext for a little *nostalgie de la bou*; and worse, a *bou* they themselves have never really experienced—free as they are to return from their pretentious ramblings to some bourgeois cantonment or other. Moreover, the Situationists' original vision of a dynamical interrelation between people and their places has also been subject—to deploy their techniques—to *détournément* (or hi-jacking) by the very interests they aimed to destroy: capitalist property developers and quasi-privatised local governments boosting their tourist destinations.

In my view, there exists an authentic tradition of psychogeography that has been practised in this archipelago for well over a century *avant la lettre*. The tap root goes deep down through the work of contemporary writers such as Iain Sinclair and the filmmakers Patrick Keiller and Julie Norris, to the likes of Arthur Machen (quoted in Sebastian Groes's Introduction); then deeper still to the English Romantics—Wordsworth, De Quincey et al.—and even deeper, to the grand peripatetic excursuses of Defoe and Addison. This tradition focuses more on what the Surrealist thinker André Breton (another of psychogeography's precursors) termed 'the frisson': that moment when the solitary stroller feels him or herself to be catapulted into a productive form of estrangement from the anthropic world. The portal to this realm—which is one, I'd argue, typified by a form of radical subjectivity—is best limned by the philosopher John Gray's observation that: 'in the city the human individual may feel themselves to be nothing but a shadow cast by the buildings'.

The Surrealists proposed their version of proto-psychogeography as a form of psychoanalysis; the therapeutic method of which was the free-association of place and space; which begs the question: what is the nature of the neurosis that afflicts our being in the contemporary built environment; the modish malaise that—to adopt the Heideggerian terminology—deflects the throwness of *dasein*? With the students at Brunel University, who, over the last decade I've attempted to introduce to the practice (and let me reiterate: psychogeography is a practice—not a field; the field is simply what we traverse), I have emphasised the importance of holding a lot of data about the built environment. Planning law, rights of way, architectural history and theory, flow dynamics, ethnography, natural history—any given place or space is also an assemblage of facts associated with each of these fields; facts that weight the subject down and further down, heavier and heavier, until apprehending the very parallax of chronology itself (for psychogeography is also a profoundly post-Einsteinian practice, allowing us to directly apprehend the relativity of space/time), in the variable ages of the buildings, the moment of letting go is arrived at.

This revolution-in-the-head, affected by emphasising through walking and sensing the very embodiment impoverished and otherwise vitiated by the man—machine matrix that entraps us, cannot be adduced by the entirely political—but neither is it a mere therapy, a 'mindfulness' of urbanity. But nothing in what I say will convince you, dear reader, until you've tried it for yourself. So, I can only recommend that you read this compendium—which includes copious amounts of the necessary data, as well as germane insights, observations and tropes—then venture out into the places and the spaces of the Black Country, there to experience the sense of radical subjectivity that so consistently informs this diverse writing.

London, UK   Will Self
June 2020

Acknowledgements

We would like to thank all project partners who collaborated with us on this olfactory adventure: the Black Country Living Museum, Wolverhampton Art Gallery, the Dudley Canal and Tunnel Trust, eBay, the Great Bridge and Wednesbury Libraries. We would like to thank all researchers and creative writers for their contribution to the Snidge Scrumpin' events, especially partners in crime Tom Mercer for crunching the numbers and Kerry Hadley-Pryce for simply being brilliant. The Centre for Transnational and Transcultural Studies and the Faculty of Arts, Business and Social Sciences at the University of Wolverhampton are thanked for their support, financially and otherwise. A special thank you goes out to Michael Eades and Amanda Phipps at the Being Human Festival for supporting and showcasing our research. The financial backers behind the Being Human Festival, the School of Advanced Studies, the British Academy and the Arts and Humanities Research Council are thanked for supporting Snidge Scrumpin'. Barry W. Smith is thanked for backing The Memory Network project and the Proust Phenomenon experiments since 2012. Ana-Karina Schneider at Sibiu University in Romania is thanked for her wonderful hosting of the

'Proust in Transylvania' event. We are grateful to Teddy Grays Sweet-shop, the curry houses of the Lye, Black Country Breweries, and the scrapyards, canals and industrial estates of the region that helped shape our olfactory cartography. We thank all our wonderful colleagues in the School of Humanities at Wolves for their dedication to the team, and the Humanities more generally.

Rob sends thanks and love to Gemma; an anchor stronger than Noah Hingley could forge.

Bas would like to thank, as always, José, for her support during his Black Country journey.

Wolverhampton, UK   Sebastian Groes
Dudley, UK   R. M. Francis
August 2020

Contents

Notes on Contributors

Esther Asprey is a Senior Teaching Fellow in the Department of Applied Linguistics at the University of Warwick. She completed a Ph.D. on Black Country English and Black Country Identity at the University of Leeds in 2007 and researches and publishes on all aspects of the Black Country dialect.

Liz Berry was born in the Black Country and now lives in Birmingham. Her first book of poems, *Black Country* (Chatto, 2014), described as a 'sooty, soaring hymn to her native West Midlands' (Guardian) was a Poetry Book Society Recommendation, received a Somerset Maugham Award and won the Geoffrey Faber Memorial Award and Forward Prize for Best First Collection 2014. Her pamphlet *The Republic of Motherhood* (Chatto, 2018) was a Poetry Book Society Pamphlet choice and the title poem won the Forward Prize for Best Single Poem 2018.

Natalie Burdett is studying for a Creative Writing Ph.D., investigating the poetry of urban place, at Manchester Metropolitan University. Her poems have been shortlisted for The London Magazine and Bridport

Prizes. Her Laureate's Choice pamphlet *Urban Drift* was published by smith|doorstop in 2018.

Anthony Cartwright is the author of five novels, the most recent of which are Iron Towns (Serpent's Tail, 2016) and The Cut (Peirene Press, 2017), a novella commissioned in response to the Brexit referendum. His work is set mostly among working-class families in his native Black Country. He is currently a writer in residence for First Story in London secondary schools and works as a tutor on the Creative Writing M.A. at City, University of London.

Stuart Connor is a Reader in Learning Futures, in the Education Observatory at the University of Wolverhampton. Faced with uncertain, contested but ultimately shared futures, Stuart's research draws on a range of approaches to examine the horizon of what are deemed probable, possible and preferable futures for learning, whilst also surfacing and questioning assumptions regarding what constitutes a desirable future and the means by which such ways of being can and should be realised.

Wendy Crickard grew up in The Lye and is the descendant of nailmakers and agricultural labourers. Her work is inspired by memories of hearing the drop hammer which started up each morning and the hand of God striking the tin chapel when Eveson's turned it into storage for the factory. With friends, she would chant 'touch collar, never swaller, never get the fever, nor yo, nor me nor any of your family' when they saw an ambulance—these childhood rhymes have influenced her poetic pacing and dynamics. She learned to read through Rupert Bear couplets and still loves good rhyme. Her work is preoccupied with the natural realms within the industrial—her local fox making regular appearances.

Narinder Dhami was born and brought up in Wolverhampton. She studied English at the University of Birmingham before becoming a primary school teacher in London. Ten years later, she left teaching to concentrate on writing. She has been a full-time children's author for the past twenty years and has published over three hundred books for readers of all ages and in a variety of genres. Her work includes the much celebrated *Bend it like Beckham*, *Superstar Babes* and *The Beautiful Game Series*.

R. M. Francis is a Lecturer in Creative and Professional Writing at the University of Wolverhampton, where he completed his Ph.D. His debut novel, Bella, was published with Wild Pressed Books in 2020, and his collection of poems, Subsidence, was published by Smokestack Books in 2020. He's published five poetry pamphlet collections and in 2019 was the inaugural David Bradshaw Writer in Residence at Oxford University.

Sebastian Groes is Professor of English Literature at the University of Wolverhampton. He has written various books, is Series Co-Editor of Contemporary Critical Perspectives (Bloomsbury) and edited volumes on Ian McEwan and Kazuo Ishiguro. Groes is the Principal Investigator of The Memory Network (www.thememorynetwork.com), an AHRC and Wellcome Trust-funded Research Network bringing together scientists, arts and humanities scholars, writers and artists. Currently, he undertakes research for the BBC's project *Novels That Shaped Our World* and works on fake news during the Corona crisis in the project TRUTH (The Rhetoric of Untruth).

Kerry Hadley-Pryce is a Visiting Lecturer at the University of Wolverhampton and the editor of The Blackcountryman magazine. Her first novel, The Black Country, published by Salt Publishing in 2015, was part of her M.A. Creative Writing at the Manchester Writing School, for which she gained a distinction and was awarded the Michael Schmidt Prize for Outstanding Achievement 2013–2014. She is currently a Ph.D. candidate at Manchester Metropolitan University researching Psychogeographic Flow and Black Country Writing. She has had several short stories published in various anthologies and online at Fictive Dream and The Incubator. Her second novel, Gamble, also published by Salt Publishing in June 2018, was shortlisted for the Encore Second Novel Award 2019.

Brendan Hawthorne is a poet, playwright, singer-songwriter, author and comic compère. He is a born and bred Black Countryman, is widely published and has held several writing residencies throughout his career. He was one of Anthony Gormley's 'Fourth Plinthers' and holds the 'Bill o Bowes' national award for best written dialect.

Kuli Kohli was born in India, married with three children and works full time. She runs Punjabi Women's Writing Group, co-coordinates Blakenhall Writers' Group and writes a regular blog for Disability Arts Online. Her debut pamphlet *Patchwork* published by Offa's Press. She's read across the West Midlands, London, Liverpool, Oswestry and via Skype to India. A guest lecturer at Humboldt University in Berlin and in December 2019 she read at The British Museum.

Paul McDonald was born in Walsall, and taught literature and creative writing at the University of Wolverhampton for twenty-five years. He now writes full time, and is the author of numerous books, including fiction, poetry and scholarship. His most recent monograph is *Allen Ginsberg: Cosmopolitan Comic* (Greenwich Exchange 2020).

Tom Mercer is a Senior Lecturer and cognitive psychologist based within the Department of Psychology at the University of Wolverhampton. Tom's main research interest is forgetting, with projects using experimental methods to examine factors responsible for the loss of memory. Much of this research examines memory for non-verbal, sensory information.

Emma Purshouse is a freelance writer, performance poet and comedienne. She is the Poet Laureate for the City of Wolverhampton. Emma performs her work nationally, and is a published author (writing both for adults and children) and poetry slam champion. She has a degree in English, and an M.A. in creative writing, and has won and been shortlisted for both local and national competitions.

List of Figures

List of Tables

1

Introduction: The Making of the Black Country

R. M. Francis and Sebastian Groes

Some say the view is crazy but you may adopt another point of view.
  —David Bowie, 'Black Country Rock', from *The Man Who Sold the World* (1970)

Off the Map: Introducing the Black Country

This book is the first to put one of Britain's most overlooked regions on the literary map whilst giving an assessment of the state of the twenty-first-century United Kingdom through a unique cross-disciplinary prism. It unites the sciences, arts and humanities with creative writing to give an insight into the condition of contemporary Britain through an analysis of one of the most fascinating and continuously disputed territories, the Black Country, a region with—we have to be honest about this—a bad rep. The post-industrial West Midlands are poor and deprived, an

R. M. Francis (✉) · S. Groes
University of Wolverhampton, Wolverhampton, UK

© The Author(s), under exclusive license to Springer
Nature Switzerland AG 2021
S. Groes et al. (eds.), *Smell, Memory, and Literature in the Black Country*,
https://doi.org/10.1007/978-3-030-57212-9_1

1

employment blackspot—and in the light of Brexit, for which the inhabitants of this region overwhelmingly voted, employment rates continue to be negatively affected.[1] It is a region of derelict buildings, of vanishing car plants and a posthumous industry through which runs a vast system of canals stemming from the early nineteenth century—and which now have lost their original, industrial function. If the Thames, in Angela Carter's words, is 'a great, wet wound', the Cut is a slasher victim.[2]

This makes the Black Country particularly suitable for poking fun at. Booker Prize-winning writer Howard Jacobson's debut novel, *Coming from Behind* (1983), written about his experience working at Wolverhampton Polytechnic (now the University of Wolverhampton), is the prime example of the satirical take the Black Country invites. In the below passage, the protagonist and Jacobson's alter ego, the Jewish English Lecturer Sefton Goldberg, compares the long-standing feud between London and the affluent south of England to Wrottesley (a fictionalised Wolverhampton):

> London, or more specifically Hampstead, was no doubt where he belonged, but it would have to wait until Sefton could enter it in triumph. In the meantime what matters was to get away from the perplexed nasal querulousness of working-class Wrottesley. The defeated and defeating poor. Other people's poverty depressed him far more than his own. O, for a beaker full of the warm south! The inane ululations of the indiscreetly well-to-do? - music, sweet music to Sefton Goldberg's ears! Their unshakeable complacency and prejudice - bliss, bliss, like the warm sun on his back, after the wrung-out despondency of Wrottesley![3]

Here, Jacobson's drawing on a lofty, mock-Keatsian lyric ode whose attempt at achieving the sublime collapses and produces mere bathos. The narrator's attitude to this geographical divide is complex: he is aware of the hypocrisy of the well-off down south, but, despite being complicit in this logic, feels empathy for the Black Country's have-nots. At the level of language, it is not only the local dialect that he's unable to understand, but neither is the posh twang of the elite. These linguistic and political complexities are something explored in depth by Esther Asprey in Chapter 10. Howardson's satire bites both ways, however, and is undercut by a human being whose state of mind is not wholly stable.

Goldberg is under the impression, for instance, that the very elements in Wrottesley are against him—personally:

> 'Bitter? Of course I'm bitter!' he repeated to himself each morning as he made his way across the ring-road which separated the Polytechnic car park from the Polytechnic. The wind was always especially sharp and bleak here and the lights were always against him. The students coming to and from lectures were dowdily dressed and looked slow-witted.[4]

We here have a satirical style heavily influenced by Dickens, using pathatic fallacy and personification of the elements to suggest a hellish experience, but of course it is Goldberg's bitter, subjective mindset that is projected onto the Black Country—and vice versa. This exchange between mind and environment makes for a highly entertaining, and quite illuminating, psychogeography.

But next to the Black Country of popular derision—an area that has suffered open, hostile bias particularly from a London-centric publishing world—there is another Black Country, a place proud of its cultural heritage, managed very successfully by several cultural institutions, spearheaded by The Black Country Living Museum that offers a unique lived experience to over 300,000 visitors each year. The history of the West Midlands music scene is impressive, bringing forth musicians from Led Zeppelin's Robert Plant to Beverley Knight MBE, whilst laying claim to being the home of heavy metal—Wolverhampton is now included in the top ten of cities with the best live music scene.[5] The area's presence and reputation have grown steadily in the popular imagination, not in the least thanks to Meera Syal's account of Black Country upbringing in *Anita and Me* (1997), Caitlin Moran's TV drama *Raised by Wolves* (2013) and *How to build a girl* (2014) and of course the wildly popular series *Peaky Blinders*, which has a considerable story to tell about Black Country history.[6] Supported by numerous literary festivals and regular events, the area is witnessing a burgeoning literary scene, including writers like Sathnam Sanghera, Anthony Cartwright, Anna Lawrence Pietroni, Kerry Hadley-Pryce, Roy McFarlane, Narinder Dhami and Liz Berry. Black Country literature has been gaining national and international recognition.

It is this extraordinary literary energy that this book maps and explores. *Snidge Scrumpin*'s uniqueness shows that the Black Country is the opposite of an area that's 'left behind': it's not only the home of original academic research, but it has a vibrant creative culture. The wider aim of this project is, then, to contribute to a process of economic and cultural regeneration and a celebration of its heritage whilst opening up pathways for a future in the second machine age.[7] We will dismantle negative stereotypes that cling to the Black Country, which is perceived to wallow in its post-industrial trauma. The region's past and the imaginative intellectual currents in the present will help the Black Country propel itself into a new, brighter future, and to help Britain confront some of its harshest contradictions with a view to telling a story of positive change and transformation.

The Black Country is a UK region with a strong cultural identity, which is rooted in the first Industrial Revolution. We may think of the Earl of Dudley's coal pits, which literally turned the countryside black— and gave the region its name. The Lavender & Co. Foundry at Hall Green, Walsall's famous tanneries and Stourbridge's glassworks are just a few of the industries that give the area its multifaceted history. But we may also think about the Goodyear Tyre and Rubber Company, which operated in Wolverhampton from 1927 till the 1970s. There is an undeniable materiality to the Black Country mindset: it is a region of manufacturing, of artisans, of stuff and things.

This region is one of contradiction and liminality. It is a borderless area, where no one is really able to define its boundaries—an old joke suggests that if one wishes to start a row, they merely need to ask 'Where is the Black Country?' What this gives rise to is a communal identity that is rooted in its industrial heritage and working-class cultures, and one that is somewhat unmappable. The Black Country is not quite north and not quite south, it is part rural and part urban, it has its own flag and set of dialects, and so much of its spirit of place is a fusion of the real and the imagined. As this book shows, this area is, in part, a made up place, an imagined construct, a heavily fictionalised world conjured up in the minds of the Black Country's writers. One particularly insightful way of understanding place is to study the lives it 'is given by writers who make and remake it in their imagination'.[8] The material structure of rationally calculable and quantifiable locations, buildings and objects as well as actions, events and people involved in them take no priority over the imagined Black Country you will find in these pages. This literary imagination and sensory exploration have a special assessment to make in understanding the workings of the private life and the personal imagination, as well as the wider concerns of the nation and the world, which, in the early twenty-first century, seems particularly critical.

Wolverhampton itself can lay claim to a quite exceptional origin story. As Wolverhampton South West's first female MP Jenny Jones notes: 'Wolverhampton is unusual not only because it was founded by a woman but because that woman managed to secure the town's safety and future prosperity at a time of great turmoil'.[9] The founding mother of Wolverhampton (a city that itself is not quite part the Black Country, or is it?), Lady Wulfruna was a Saxon noblewoman who lived in the tenth century AD, when the Saxon England consisted of seven warring kingdoms. The Vikings were not done with England yet either, and the history books speak of a great battle between the Danes and the Kingdom of Mercia, knows as the Battle of Tettenhall in 910 AD (though it might have also been at Wednesbury). A couple of decades later, Olaf Guthfrithson, led a fierce and bloody assault on Tamworth that resulted in the capture and imprisonment of Lady Wulfruna, who was held for ransom. She was a member of a powerful Mercian family, and held property and land. After payment of 'Danegeld', Wulfruna gave birth to two sons who went on to be very powerful (Aelfhelm and Wulfric Spott). In 985, King Aethelred granted lands at a place referred to as a *Heantun*—Saxon for 'high place'—to Wulfruna. The land contained streams, springs, fields and marshes, livestock, farms, mills, other buildings and their serfs. It is at this point that the area later known as the Black Country first enters the annals—a world wholly different from the Black Country as we know it today. As R. M. Francis writes in his chapter on place-identity: 'Indeed, as we know so little factual details of this pre-Norman Britain, as so much of the history is recorded through hear-say and Norman propaganda, it's impossible to make an authentic and rational claim about this. The Mercian heritage of the region becomes a myth; a narrative linked to a place. The sense of place is part-fact and part-fable'. These stories, from the semi-mythical past of England, afford contemporary writers a host of material to work with—Anthony Cartwright mentions the battle of Woden's Field in 910 AD—it is not just the post-industrial past that holds up a mirror to us.

Making Sense of the Black Country

One key claim this book makes: it is precisely because of its intense industrial heritage that the Black Country is so integrated into the sensory—and sensual—lives of its inhabitants. It is almost as if, when pricking up one's ear, you can still hear men shouting in the mills and mines; you can taste smoke in the air; and you can smell the coal clogging up your nose. As R. M. Francis notes: '*We're stuck in the muck of it all*'.

Indeed, the angle that unites the various perspectives in this book is an interest in the relationship to the ways in which smell is deeply intertwined with (childhood) memory, as Marcel Proust explored in the first part of *In Search of Lost Time* (1913). As Groes and Mercer explain in more detail in their chapter, the so-called Proust Phenomenon was occasioned by a moment when the writer dipped a madeleine cake in his tea, and the taste and, particularly, the smell transports him back to his childhood in the fictional town Combray. Since the publication of the novel, scientists and scholars have been intrigued by this phenomenon and have been trying to understand how this exactly works. The Memory Network, a research network that brings scientists, scholars and writers together to rethink how memory works in the twenty-first century, undertook a number of experiments to show that smell triggers more emotion and intense childhood memories compared to auditory, visual and textual stimuli and that we remember images better if they are associated with a smell (see Chapter 7).

Smell is unique because it evokes intense and emotional (childhood) memories (Willander and Larsson 2006). The neural basis for smell is also unique. Olfaction is the only sense that bypasses the thalamic relay and has primary access to regions of the brain typically found to be active during emotional processing (the amygdala), long-term memory formation (the hippocampus) and higher order cognitive reasoning (orbitofrontal cortex). It is this unusual neural makeup that has led many to speculate on the unique access olfaction has to memory, emotion and higher order cognition (Soudry et al. 2011). As well as an extraordinary biological basis olfaction is extraordinary intertwined into human culture, but, paradoxically, also the most underappreciated of our senses. In our modern culture, visual stimulation is dominant and sanitisation is everywhere: we mask smells and artificially scent spaces and bodies. The result is a loss of smell awareness, which is dangerous as smell is connected to our delicately balanced sensory system, and to depression (Kohli et al. 2016; Taalman et al. 2018), stress levels (Angelucci et al. 2014), sexual attraction (Verhaege et al. 2013; Collins and Whillans 2018). Amnosmics, parosmics and ageing people whose sense of smell is impaired have mental health and identity issues because their access to memory (Herz 2016) or affective states (Weber and Heuberger 2008) is blocked.

More recently, The Memory Network reinvented its Proust Phenomenon research by exploring how a specific place is connected to smells and (childhood) memories. The identity of is not simply defined by the material structures and spatial laws that define it, but there is what we call a 'sensory footprint' that characterises a specific geography. At the Snidge Scrumpin' experiments, we tested whether Black Country locals had a better ability to name the smells that we had selected after a media campaign, with input from a panel of experts. We also wanted to know if there was a specificity to the memories evoked by regional smells in Black Country denizens. The result of these experiments can be read in Chapter 7.

The Proust Phenomenon is a great example showing that literature is capable of allowing different disciplines to speak to one another. Neuroscience can explain why smell is a strong trigger (olfaction has direct connection with the limbic system involved in generating emotions and memory), and psychology can show which stimuli have particularly vivid and emotional effects, but literature has an equally important role to play in revealing how memory works. We might argue that without literature, emotions remain silenced, that literature is the key to unlocking the voice of those emotions.

Indeed, the Proust Phenomenon's wider significance in not only to do with nostalgia for our personal, subjective past: by triggering strong, emotive childhood memories, we are being reconnected with our former selves, with the selves that we (may) have forgotten. This process is beneficial because it gives us a different vantage point upon our lives—affording us the possibility of perspective and contemplation. These moments confront us with our younger selves, perhaps different, more innocent, and thus asking questions about selfhood and causation—we come to wonder how we ended up where we are now—what life choices, what motives and desires have brought us where we find ourselves today. More sensory explorations of childhood memories and life trajectories can be found in the pieces of creative writing that punctuate this book, including Stuart Connor's three striking vignettes in his chapter on Black Country Futures.

Indeed, what all contributions in this book enact is to enhance a growing smell awareness in our contemporary society. Speaking to people about smell is always a little embarrassing. Just the mention of the word 'smell' makes people smirk. Yet, smell is extremely important, as we've seen above. Smell is related to depression, stress, pleasure, survival and sexuality. There is a long history of the politicisation of smell, whereby the working classes, as George Orwell has shown on more than one occasion, were discriminated against via their association with bad odours. The history of colonial oppression made use of an olfactory exclusion based on (imagined) hygiene and sanitary ideology. The many unresolved twenty-first-century debates about our relationship to nature, and on freedom and social injustice include a sensory emancipation: we can only find a new, fairer order of things if we actively accept an inclusive, and socially diverse agenda that unpicks biases. This means a continuous deconstruction of all hegemonies, including sensory ones: the dominance of vision in a culture dominated by the screen must be balanced out by sensory restoration that includes a focus on smell. The Corona crisis challenges how we live, think, love, travel and asks us to reconsider our priorities on all levels of life, and smell had an important role to play: anosmia—smell impairment or smell loss—is one of the warning signs of Covid-19 infection.[10] More awareness of smell will benefit our societies, also, and perhaps particularly, in the twenty-first century.

Darkest England and the Post-pastoral

The Black Country is not unique in its otherness. From Scunthorpe to the north of England to London's East End, many areas outside the affluent north London postcodes were, or continue to be, in decline. However, the Black Country is a particularly useful example, offering signs of liminality or marginality that many other regions do not. The Black Country is not quite urban—not quite rural; it's made up of a strange mix of green and grey spaces; much of its cultural identity is formed from its industrial heritage, but most of this is now obsolete, ruined, built over by retail sites and enterprise zones. All these things are typical of a post-industrial environment, examples can be seen in the suburbs of Gateshead and Glasgow. The Black Country has three further signs, making it exemplar for investigating the post-industrial and the liminal: it's not quite north and not quite south; it sits in the shadow of its bigger, wealthier, more successful brother, Birmingham; and most importantly, it's a defined state with its own name, flag, set of dialects, heritage, but it has no fixed boundary. If we find ourselves in this in-between, borderless space, what might that do to sense of self? Might it give rise to liminal identity and/or experience? Is it possible that this liminal identity/experience is particular to the region? We deal with this in terms of Harold Proshansky's Place-Identity in Chapter 13.

Its difference is, in fact, symptomatic of the effects of a long history of capitalism and politics of a political and cultural metropolitan elite that has for centuries exploited natural resources and human bodies. Raymond Williams's idea of 'darkest London'—by which he meant London's East End, is an idea that can be replicated across space and time.[11] Williams spoke about a place 'of darkness, of oppression, of crime and squalor, or reduced humanity', and much of Williams's observations were and are suitable to understanding the non-metropolitan spaces outside Britain's cities.[12] Williams shows that the diametrical opposition of city and country is a worn-out ruse: for a long time, critics and writers have observed that 'Old England' and its timeless rural associations and organic structure laid down in sentimental pastoral narratives have disappeared, though the Edenic mythology as well as the nostalgia for the past, have remained. This is what Williams calls a problem of perspective: at one and the same time, we long back for an idealised past whilst being confronted with a post-pastoral reality. It is this mythology of loss that characterises many literatures, but the English one especially—but we need to learn to take on, or at least acknowledge, a new perspective to truly understand what is happening to non-metropolitan spaces in modernity, and dismantle the diametrical opposition that exists purely in the mythology of thinkers and (Romantic) writers, from Thomas More to Wordsworth. The Black Country's position and situation is, of course, akin to London's East End. As Kerry Hadley-Pryce reminds us, in this region we find 'that awkward kind of Black Country darkness'.[13]

The development of Black Country literature accelerates during the industrial revolution, and comes into its own in the latter part of the Victorian era and in the early twentieth century. Its title inspired by the 'abundance of ironworks and furnaces in the Black Country [that] produced smoke and debris which darkened the landscape', Paul McDonald's *Fiction from the Furnace* (2002) was the first academic study to put the literary history of the area on the map.[14] The book takes us on a tour that includes writers including David Christie Murray; Ellen Thorneycroft Fowler; Francis Brett Young; George Woden; Henry Treece; Maurice Wiggin; John Petty and Archie Hill—writers that are given a new, linguistic assessment by Asprey in Chapter 10. What binds all these writers, who observed the Black Country during its industrial heyday, was that the area excited the imagination, both praising and condemning, both enthusiasm and tacit reservation. It was McDonald who pioneered in mapping and analysing the ambivalent, confused response that the Black Country triggered in the writerly mind.[15]

Ian Haywood discusses this post-pastoral reality in *Working-Class Fictions* (1997), focusing on literature from non-metropolitan and post-industrial places. In his readings of writers such as Alan Sillitoe, he addresses the distinct and difficult cultural, political and geographic shifts that took place in the United Kingdom's industrial heartlands. He says,

> a colossal transfer of economic power from the public to the private
> sector has taken place in Britain. Traditional working-class communities

organised around largescale manufacturing industry have all but disappeared from British social life; the social imagery of such communities has become nostalgic, while the 'affluent' working-class has been heralded by conservative politicians as evidence of a new 'classlessness' [resulting in] the accelerated the fragmentation of class-consciousness [...] the ideological effect of submerging working-class identity (or significant fractions of it) into a heterogenous, proletarianized underclass of alienated social groups, defined by their economic unproductiveness and an inability to participate fully in society.[16]

We have seen this industrial and post-industrial tradition in the work of many different writers, but the Black Country has not only generated realist fiction: even—or, perhaps, especially, the weird fiction of Arthur Machen found the area fruitful source of inspiration. Consider Arthur Machen's *The Secret Glory* (1922), a novel about a young man, Ambrose Meyrick, in search of mystical transcendence, starting out in a harsh Public School in the Black Country in the fictional place called 'Lupton'. Here is a poignant description of the Black Country's condition during its industrial heyday, when Ambrose meditates upon the Midlands landscape:

> So he stood, wrapt in his meditations and in his ecstasy, by the bridge over the Midland line from Lupton to Birmingham. Behind him were the abominations of Lupton: the chimneys vomiting black smoke faintly in honour of the Sabbath; the red lines of the workmen's streets advancing into the ugly fields; the fuming pottery kilns, the hideous height of the boot factory. And before him stretched the unspeakable scenery of the eastern Midlands, which seems made for the habitation of English Nonconformists—dull, monotonous, squalid, the very hedgerows cropped and trimmed, the trees looking like rows of Roundheads, the farmhouses as uninteresting as suburban villas. On a field near at hand a scientific farmer had recently applied an agreeable mixture consisting of superphosphate of lime, nitrate of soda and bone meal. The stink was that of a chemical works or a Texel cheese.[17]

Science and artifice have replaced nature, the untouched, whilst a definite, rigid class division is making itself in the landscape. Ambrose is fully able to interpret what he sees, but he is appalled by what both worlds offer to him: the unsound, sickly work of industry is hateful, but the remaining agricultural world is not only 'uninteresting' but even ineffable. In fact, the 'scientific farmer', who tampers with the land, shows that both are equally corrupt. There is no choice.

The imagination can, however, transcend these base, material conditions by means of an act of literary alchemy. In an otherworldly scene that starts off mundane, Ambrose overlooks the Black Country landscape, a wild, bare country, the sky hidden by livid clouds. Yet, just a moment after, the following happens:

> Suddenly there was, as it were, a cry far away in the shadowy silence, and Machen, 37 to rustle before a shrilling wind that rose as the night came down. At this summons the heavy clouds broke up and dispersed, fleeting across the sky, and the pure heaven appeared with the last rose flush of the sunset dying from it, and there shone the silver light of the evening star. Ambrose's heart was drawn up to this light as he gazed: he saw that the star grew greater and greater; it advanced towards him through the air; its beams pierced to his soul as if they were the sound of a silver trumpet. An ocean of white splendour flowed over him: he dwelt within the star.[18]

The surface materiality crumbles and opens up numinous awe. This is not a Joycean epiphany, but an unspeakable moment of the Sublime as formulated by Edmund Burke in *A Philosophical Enquiry into the Origin of Our Ideas of the Sublime and Beautiful* (1757). The realist, 'authentic' vision makes way for a Romantic, lyrical mental dreamscape composed of supernatural elements. Machen explores the mystical, perhaps apocalyptic belief that beyond the superficial world of matter lies a curious, mysterious world—an aesthetic that has the power to fascinate and annihilate us. By lifting the veil, by unconcealing as Stuart Connor calls it in his chapter on Black Country Futures, we could see beyond this world of stuff and things and explore self-sacrifice that could lead to transformation—but the point is that beyond the worldly matter—of which the Black Country has more than plenty—lies mental and spiritual emancipation, liberation.

This sense of seeking out sublime otherness in the dark industrial abyss continues into contemporary explorations of literary Black Country too. Writers in this collection convey the Black Country and its characters as being in positions of flux, contradiction and transition. The places described in these works are ones where urban decay and the weeds of semi-rural space compete for territory. These writers share a sense of pride and nostalgia for the area's industrial heritage and working-class ethics, as well as a sense of despair towards the ruins, waste grounds and new enterprises that now replace it. Using the local area, its history and vernacular these authors expose their characters and readership to abject and uncanny experiences. In terms of cultural and geographical context, and in thematic content, they provide a sense of the border-less, the ghostly, the weird. Their settings are places that are not secure but ones that draw characters in, spaces and situations that are, in equal measure, inviting and homely as well as threatening.

Cartwright, for example, uses the rich and deep-rooted social struc-tures and culture of working-class Dudley to explore wider political issues and social concerns. The fictional adaptations of Dudley (or 'Cinder-heath', as he calls it) and its inhabitants become the microcosm for questions of class, gender, race, desire, alienation, love and hate. He explores these issues by depicting cultures and characters that are in tran-sition and borderless. In his third novel, *How I Killed Margaret Thatcher* (2013), we're transported to Dudley during Thatcher's first Conserva-tive term as Prime Minister—one that was set to make irreversible and uncompromising changes to the industrial and working-class areas of the United Kingdom.[19] This novel indicates Cartwright's interest in depicting what made Dudley and its people post-industrial, as being in a state of upheaval and unrest. The action in the novel traces lives and cultures that have been forced into liminality, and because of this, need to re-establish their sense of place, class, identity and history.

As Paul McDonald notes in his chapter on contemporary Black Country literature: 'By far the most popular Black Country based stories of the past three decades have come from two of the region's British-Asian writers, Meera Syal and Sathnam Sanghra, for whom representations of the region are linked to issues of race and identity'. In this book, we see British-Asian by Narinder Dhami and Kuli Kholi, suggesting how the immigrant experience has added an important new perspective on the Black Country. We may also think of Black British poet Roy McFarlane, whose poetry has the cyclical at its heart as he explores familial, ethnic and regional identity as things that are constantly shifting or adapting. For McFarlane, identity and the search for truth or being are incessant resurgences. McFarlane explores episodes and rites of passage that lead to transformation, and how in turn these bring about further need for change.[20] It is a Christian ethic, following the example of Jesus' resurrection and seeing baptism as a form of rebirth.[21] McFarlane's cycles of understanding contain another layer of liminality too, investigating the in-between nature of adopted people and importantly bringing race to the fore.[22] McFarlane deals with his own adoption in these confessional poems, thinking about himself as within and outside of the family. The narrative arch of the collection leads the reader through what Turner called *Limen*: experiences of moving away from one sense of being and becoming another. This collection explores race in similar ways; McFarlane recognises the protracted liminal positions of the Windrush Generation and their subsequent ancestors, asking pertinent questions about Black British identity, set within the borderless region of the Black Country. As Carney points out, 'it is the idea of finding home that reigns supreme, with Wolverhampton – aka "That place just off the M6" – taking centre stage'.[23]

Liz Berry's Forward Prize-winning poetry collection, *The Black Country* (2014), explores her birthplace in explicitly bestial and sexual terms, focussing on the interplay of place and growth, language and learning, organic and machine. Berry uses the region's industrial heritage, its borderlessness to create metaphors for sensuality, sexuality and for discussing ideas of coming into being. Many of the poems deal with coming into being in some way; in terms of understanding selfhood through language; in sexual terms; and in terms of investigating queer or uncanny experiences. Her work is fixated on situations or moods where the characters are in-between states.[24] Berry is preoccupied with the dark, filthy aspects of the Black Country and how she perceives these as connecting with sensuality and eroticism—hinting at a specifically located sexuality.

A Brexit Psychogeography

Brexit is the revenge of the unresolved mental crisis caused not only by the decline of Empire but also by postmodernism's spatio-temporal politics on the United Kingdom. The Black Country's situation should be contextualised within a global condition that has affected many areas across the world. Indeed, the Black Country is Brexit heartland that is shared with, for example, the disaffected places in the United States that put Trump in power. These places often experienced their heyday during the industrial revolution, but were abandoned by political leaders in the 1980s.

Much of the recent fictional writing about Brexit is set in the Black Country, from Hadley-Pryce's *The Black Country* (2015) and *Gamble* (2018) and Anthony Cartwright's Brexit exploration *The Cut* (2017) to Jonathan Coe's *Middle England* (2018). Look for instance at Liz Berry's poem 'Wolverhampton Central Library, Children's Library, 1980s' (2018): here we encounter a seemingly nostalgic, Proustian return to a childhood safe space triggered by smell:

> The Black Country she was born into is already lost, shelved mournfully and thankfully on tissue thin pages in the Local History section. Industry and Genius: A Fable. Now it's the work of words and books, a different kind of mining from the dark.

Berry's analysis here is complex, and chimes in with the double perspective Williams identifies in *The Country and the City* (1973): buried beneath the nostalgia is something 'feral'; the leaving behind of the industrial era comes with a mixture of lament and relief. The Enlightenment project ('Industry and Genius') has turned out to be a ruse (even though destroying a harmonic sense organic community), but Berry's persona has invented a new goal in the world of words—though even this remains something of an uncertain activity that sheds not much light into the confused state of life in the early twenty-first century. This offers a post-pastoral perspective on the present.

Much of contemporary Black Country writing is central to understanding what Brexit really is: a complex, confusing, irate process of disaffection that has made visible wounds—the slasher victim comes to mind—that is unlikely to heal easily nor quickly because this trauma and alienation run so deeply. Black Country literature offers a Brexit psychogeography, tales of trauma and alienation, of feeling 'left behind', in terms of time and space. The phrase 'left behind', firstly, to do with a temporal condition. After the collapse of heavy and manufacturing industry that comes with the decline of Empire, regions such as the Black Country failed to receive the financial incentive that would enable them to step into the second machine age. Whereas East London, Norwich, Manchester and Liverpool, a city where one could buy a house in the Kensington area for one pound in the noughties, were gentrified just after the millennial turn. A city such as Wolverhampton is only now, in the late 2010s and early 2020s, receiving major investment from the government to change its infrastructure and civic buildings. This time lag has created a strange schizophrenic consciousness: still living in the ruins of its industrial past, the Black Country is not past nor quite present because the derelict buildings point to a history that no longer is quite here. So, for the time being, the Black Country puts time out of joint: perhaps the Black Country isn't posthumous, but has experienced, in Steven Connor's words, a 'pseudo-death': 'there is nothing but mortality in ruins, but it is too late for ruins to die, they are too old, too ruinous'.[25]

Next to temporal alienation, we see a similar movement in terms of space and place. Jameson defined the postmodern condition spatially, architecturally, and because of the time lag, the Black Country preserves the physical ruins of the first industrial revolutions. And the buildings in the Black Country Living Museum, carefully dis- and reassembled, brick by brick, together with the actors inhabiting historical roles provides a perfect Baudrillardian simulacrum. Rem Koolhaas calls this 'junkspace':

> Junkspace is what remains after modernization has run its course, or, more precisely, what coagulates while modernization is in progress, its fallout. Modernization has a rational program: to share the blessings of science, universally. Junkspace is its apotheosis, or meltdown ... Although the individual parts are the outcome of brilliant inventions. Lucidly planned by human intelligence, boosted by infinite computation, their

sum spells the end of the Enlightenment, its resurrection a farce, a low-grade purgatory.[26]

In this sense, the predicament of Detroit's car manufacturing industry in the late nineties and early noughties, or the abandoned industrial site of Hackney Wick (gentrified for the London Olympics, 2012), is largely the same as that of Wolverhampton, where the remainder of heavy industry is disappearing.[27]

Yet, the Black Country's different from Detroit and London as it is not distinctly a city or metropolis: consisting of four metropolitan boroughs that have to a large extent grown together into a conglomeration that isn't quite urban nor rural or village either. It is a single continuous town connected by a 14-mile road between Wolverhampton and Birmingham. The region is unlike London, which to a large extent kept its organic, medieval blueprint—and caused Will Self to call it a 'might ergot fungus, erupting from the very crust of the earth, a growing, mutating thing, capable of taking on the most fantastic profusion of shapes'.[28] The Black Country resembles what J. G. Ballard called, in the case of the Mediterranean beach resorts from Gibraltar to Glyfada Beach, a curious 'linear city' that reaches out rhizomically from Birmingham to Dudley (the unofficial capital of the Black Country) and from Stourbridge to Walsall.[29]

The Black Country can and cannot be conceptualised within the 'traditional' (if psychogeography can ever be 'traditional') psychogeographical rules. The concept 'psychogeography' was invented by the leader of the Situationist Internationale, Guy Debord, to playfully, wittily resist and subvert the modern city as a material structure that had a detrimental effect on the human mind and behaviour. Debord set out to expose and subvert the increased technocratic rationality that found its greatest expression in modern Paris by engaging in ludic, anti-scientific activities. Debord noted that below the pavement you would find a beach, a leisure space that would work against the strictures of capitalist labour, whilst a new form of experimental walking, the *dérive* (the drift), would map the varied ambiances through transient passages of urban spaces. Another subversive spatial strategy was *détournement*, which involved turning or diverting spatial expressions of capitalism against itself; it often involved buildings, streets, pavements and parks, which were ironised and/or reinvented through performative and linguistic interventions. Creative mapping and subversive appropriation of the emotional guides were dissenting acts that exposed the machinery of modernity in which the individual was dehumanised.

If psychogeography was originally intended to evade and criticise the power of technocratic capitalism upon the human mind and body, the Black Country to a degree needs an anti-psychogeography because to large degree central powers have *not* cared for these regions. This is exactly why places like the Black Country can feel liberating—as Machen anticipated 100 years ago: there is a sense it is (just about) outside the law, and you feel, cheekily, you might just get away with causing trouble just a bit more than in densely regulated, hyper-observed places in urbanity—a Wild West of sorts.

Perhaps not much longer. Investors are moving in, the government is contributing to the gentrification of the region, cultural enterprises such as the Black Country Living Museum and the Wolverhampton Art Gallery attracting more and more visitors year on year, the literary and artistic scene is booming. Inaugurated in 2019, the Black Country Studies Centre is evidence of the area's growing self-consciousness about itself.[30] The region seems to be at a tipping point. The Black Country is late in its awakening from its post-industrial slumber, but not too late.

Notes

1. See 'West Midlands Is Now an Employment Blackspot, Says Thinktank', *The Guardian*, 12 December 2016. See: https://www.theguardian.com/business/2016/dec/12/west-midlands-employment-blackspot-thinktank-resolution [Accessed 9 August 2019].
2. Angela Carter, 'Iain Sinclair: *Downriver*', in *Expletives Deleted* (London: Chatto & Windus, 1992), 120.
3. Howard Jacobson, *Coming from Behind* (London: Vintage, 2011), Loc. 116. Originally published by Chatto & Windus in 1983.
4. Jacobson, Loc. 253.

5. See 'Wolverhampton Hits Top 10 for Best Love Music Scene', *City of Wolverhampton Council* website, 15 July, 2016. See https://www.wolver hampton.gov.uk/news/wolverhampton-hits-top-10-best-live-music-scene [Accessed 9 August 2019].

6. See Carl Chinn, *Peaky Blinders: The Real Story of Birminghm's Most Notorious Gang* (London: John Blake, 2019).

7. Andrew McAfee and Erik Brynjolfsson *The Second Machine Age: Work, Progress, and Prosperity in a Time of Brilliant Technologies* (New York and London: Norton, 2014).

8. Sebastian Groes, *The Making of London* (London: Palgrave, 2011), 1.

9. See Jenny Jones, 'Lady Wulfruna: Wolverhampton's Founding Mother', http://www.historywebsite.co.uk/articles/wulfruna/wulfruna01.htm [Accessed 15 March 2020].

10. See Sarah Boseley, 'Thousands of Covid-19 Cases Missed Due to Late Warning on Smell Loss', *The Guardian*, 18 May 2020. https://www.the guardian.com/world/2020/may/18/uk-coronavirus-tests-advised-for-peo ple-who-lose-taste-or-smell [Accessed 18 May 2020].

11. Raymond Williams, *The Country and the City* (London: Chatto and Windus, 1973), 221.

12. Williams, 227.

13. Kerry Hadley-Pryce, *The Black Country* (Cromer: Salt, 2015), 13.

14. Paul McDonald, *Fiction from the Furnace: A Hundred Years of Black Country Writing* (Sheffield: Sheffield University Press, 2002), 8.

15. McDonald, 12.

16. Ian Haywood, *Working-Class Fiction: From Chartism to Trainspotting* (Tavistock: Northcote, 1997), 140–141.

17. Arthur Machen, *The Secret Glory* (New York: Knopf, 1922), 58.

18. Machen, 24.

19. When asked about why he chose to deal with Thatcher's government and that era Cartwright said, 'Dudley went through a real, real terrible time during that period, like loads of other towns up and down the country [...] with industries being killed, [Cartwright gestures] right, this way of life isn't going to happen anymore'. See: Fiction Uncovered, *Anthony Cartwright interviewed by Courttia Newland*, Published 31 May 2013, Fiction Uncovered, https://www.youtube.com/watch?v=rK5 kLFdAYbs [Accessed 16 March 2016], unpaginated.

20. In a recent interview he said: 'There's certainly an emphasis on a circle of life, that there are no endings, they only feed into another beginning, like the seasons, winter is not an ending but it's a preparation for the spring to

come'. 'In The Booklight—Roy McFarlane & Beginning with Your Last Breath' (an interview with Sarah James), 2016, http://www.sarah-james.co.uk/?p=7636 [Accessed 03 May 2018], unpaginated.

21. Bridget Minamore notices this in her review of McFarlane's collection: '*Beginning with your last breath* is cyclical in nature, and, ultimately, comes back to the fact we have been told one man's story. A tale of motherhood, music, home and love; of finding out more about yourself, your home and your mother, despite already seemingly knowing all three. However, all stories must come to an end – but here, we see, an end is also a new beginning. See Bridget Minamore, 'Review: Beginning with Your Last Breath by Roy McFarlane', *Poetry School*, https://poetryschool.com/reviews/review-beginning-last-breath-roy-mcfarlane/ [Accessed 03 May 2018], unpaginated.

22. Rachel Carney points this out, saying, 'the book holds together through the shared themes of identity, family, love and loss, in the context of racial tension and cultural change'. See: Rachel Carney, 'Review: Beginning with Your Last Breath by Roy McFarlane', *Created to Read*, 2017, https://createdtoread.com/poetry-beginning-with-your-last-breath-roy-mcfarlane/ [Accessed 03 May 2018], unpaginated.

23. Carney, 'Review: Beginning with Your Last Breath by Roy McFarlane'.

24. In a recent interview Berry discusses the filth and darkness in the region and her writing, saying that exploring this is a 'very subversive idea in lots of ways because it's both repulsive and fascinating and delightful […] I suppose it's where the dark side of the erotic can be found, especially sensuality and women's sensuality […] people have talked about it as earthy and I think earthy is as close as they can get to saying sort of the dirt, the filth or the muck of it'. See: 'Brave New Reads', *Jonathan Morley Interviews Poet Liz Berry*, Published 18 August 2015, WCNOnline, https://www.youtube.com/watch?v=oD3-jpcHaSE [Accessed 16 March 2016], unpaginated.

25. Steven Connor, 'Sufficiently Decayed', a talk given at the Frieze Art Fair, London, 15 October, 2006. See http://stevenconnor.com/ruins/ruins.pdf [Accessed 9 August 2019].

26. Rem Koolhaas, 'Junkspace', *October* 100, Obsolesence (Spring, 2002): 175–190; 175.

27. See Michael Chanan' and George Steinmetz's *Detroit: Ruin of a City* (Artfilms, 2005).

28. Will Self, *My Idea of Fun: A Cautionary Tale* (London: Penguin, 1993), 304.

29. J. G. Ballard, *Vermillion Sands* (London: Penguin: Random House, 2016), 7.
30. The Black Country Studies Centre is a partnership between the University of Wolverhampton and the Black Country Living Museum that aims to bring together multidisciplinary research on the Black Country. See http://blackcountrystudiescentre.co.uk [Access 13 March 2020].

Works Cited

Angelucci, F. L., V. V. Silva, C. Dal Pizzol, L. G. Spir, C. E. O. Praes and H. Maibach. 'Physiological Effect of Olfactory Stimuli Inhalation in Humans: An Overview', *International Journal of Cosmetic Science 36* (2014), 117–123. https://doi.org/10.1111/ics.12096.

Ballard, J. G. *Vermillion Sands* (London: Penguin: Random House, 2016).

Berry, Liz. 'Brave New Reads', *Jonathan Morley Interviews Poet Liz Berry*, Published 18 August 2015, WCNOnline, https://www.youtube.com/watch?v=oD3-jpcHaSE [Accessed 16 March 2016].

Boseley, Sarah. 'Thousands of Covid-19 Cases Missed Due to Late Warning on Smell Loss', *The Guardian*, 18 May, 2020. https://www.theguardian.com/world/2020/may/18/uk-coronavirus-tests-advised-for-people-who-lose-taste-or-smell [Accessed 18 May 2020].

Carter, Angela. 'Iain Sinclair: *Downriver*', in *Expletives Deleted* (London: Chatto & Windus, 1992).

Cartwright, Anthony. 'Fiction Uncovered', *Anthony Cartwright interviewed by Courttia Newland*, Published 31 May 2013, Fiction Uncovered, https://www.youtube.com/watch?v=rK5kLFdAYbs [Accessed 16 March 2016], unpaginated.

Chanan, Michael and Steinmetz, George. *Detroit: Ruin of a City* (Artfilms, 2005).

Chinn, Carl. *Peaky Blinders: The Real Story of Birminghm's Most Notorious Gang* (London: John Blake, 2019).

Connor, Steven. 'Sufficiently Decayed', a talk given at the Frieze Art Fair, London, 15 October, 2006. See http://stevenconnor.com/ruins/ruins.pdf [Accessed 9 August 2019].

Groes, Sebastian. *The Making of London* (London: Palgrave, 2011).

Hadley-Pryce, Kerry. *The Black Country* (Cromer: Salt, 2015).

Haywood, Ian. *Working Class Fiction: From Chartism to Trainspotting*, (Devon: Northcote House Publishing Ltd, 1997)

Herz, Rachel S. 'The Role of Odor-Evoked Memory in Psychological and Physiological Health', *Brain sciences 6*(3) (2016): 22. https://doi.org/10.3390/brainsci6030022.

Jacobson, Howard. *Coming from Behind* (London: Vintage, 2011).

Jones, Jenny. 'Lady Wulfruna: Wolverhampton's Founding Mother', http://www.historywebsite.co.uk/articles/wulfruna/wulfruna01.htm [Accessed 15 March, 2020].

Kohli, Preeti, Zachary M. Soler, Shaun A. Nguyen, John S. Muus and Rodney J. Schlosser. 'The Association Between Olfaction and Depression: A Systematic Review', *Chemical Senses 41*(6) (2016): 479–486.

Koolhaas, Rem. 'Junkspace', *October* 100, Obsolesence (Spring, 2002).

Machen, Arthur. *The Secret Glory* 95, (New York: Arnold A. Knopf, 1922).

McAfee, Andrew and Brynjolfsson, Erik. *The Second Machine Age: Work, Progress, and Prosperity in a Time of Brilliant Technologies* (New York and London: Norton, 2014).

McDonald, Paul. *Fiction from the Furnace: A Hundred Years of Black Country Writing* (Sheffield: Sheffield University Press, 2002).

McFarlane, Roy. 'The Booklight—Roy McFarlane & Beginning with Your Last Breath' (an interview with Sarah James), 2016, http://www.sarah-james.co.uk/?p=7636 [Accessed 03 May 2018].

Minamore, Bridget. 'Review: Beginning with Your Last Breath by Roy McFarlane', *Poetry School*, https://poetryschool.com/reviews/review-beginning-last-breath-roy-mcfarlane/ [Accessed 03 May 2018].

Self, Will. *My Idea of Fun: A Cautionary Tale* (London: Penguin, 1993).

Soudry, Y., C. Lemogne, D. Malinvaud, S. M. Consoli, and P. Bonfils. 'Olfactory System and Emotion: Common Substrates', *European Annals of Otorhinolaryngology, Head and Neck Diseases 128*(1) (2011): 18–23. https://doi.org/10.1016/j.anorl.2010.09.007. Epub 2011 Jan 11. PMID: 21227767.

Taalman, H., C. Wallace and R. Milev. 'Olfactory Functioning and Depression: A Systematic Review', *Front Psychiatry 8* (2018): 190. https://doi.org/10.3389/fpsyt.2017.00190. PMID: 29033860; PMCID: PMC5627007.

Weber, Sandra T. and Eva Heuberger. 'The Impact of Natural Odors on Affective States in Humans', *Chemical Senses, 33*(5) (2008): 441–447. https://doi.org/10.1093/chemse/bjn011.

'West Midlands Is Now an Employment Blackspot, Says Thinktank', *The Guardian*, 12 December 2016, https://www.theguardian.com/business/2016/dec/12/west-midlands-employment-blackspot-thinktank-resolution [Accessed 9 August 2019].

Willander, Johan and Larsen, Maria. 'Smell Your Way Back to Childhood: Autobiographical Odour Memory', *Psychonomic Bulletin & Review 13*(2) (2006): 240–244.

Williams, Raymond. *The Country and the City* (London: Chatto and Windus, 1973).

'Wolverhampton Hits Top 10 for Best Love Music Scene', *City of Wolverhampton Council* website, 15 July 2016. See https://www.wolverhampton.gov.uk/news/wolverhampton-hits-top-10-best-live-music-scene [Accessed 9 August 2019].

2

Wolverhampton Central Library, Children's Library, 1980s

Liz Berry

The smell of it, even now, is like being stroked behind the knees, it makes me buckle.

A wood in September: the warm singe of heat on bark, sweat, leaf-smoke, the air all of a sudden freckled with dust, and me kneeling between the stacks, face hidden in the leaves of a book.

I'm in that formless time before school, waiting for her to finish work. My mom, the librarian. In that humming forest of books, she moves gently as a root. Her scent is everywhere amongst the stacks: the tea on her tongue, the vinegar tang of her feet as she slips off her pinching shoes behind the counter, her perfume, *anais anais*, white lilies over leather and wood. She is a pale bloom in the dim hush between the shelves and swaying ladders, the soft sh shhh of the date stamp.

Her quiet world has the yellow smell that yearning has, the dreaming yellow of thousands of thumbed pages and cracked spines. The smell of being saved. There's something feral there too, something alive, in

L. Berry (✉)
Birmingham, UK

© The Author(s), under exclusive license to Springer
Nature Switzerland AG 2021
S. Groes et al. (eds.), *Smell, Memory, and Literature in the Black Country*,
https://doi.org/10.1007/978-3-030-57212-9_2

the beanbags and flattened moss green carpet—a zing of ammonia: sucked pear drops, the little animal reek of piss, small unwashed bodies uncurling into the light.

The Black Country she was born into is already lost, shelved mournfully and thankfully on tissue thin pages in the Local History section. Industry and Genius: A Fable. Now it's the work of words and books, a different kind of mining from the dark. And here is her child is waiting for her, swinging her legs on a wooden chair, but still—for a moment longer than is needed—she kneels amongst the hardbacks and buries her face in the yellow winged moth of a book, breathing its smell of paper and binding; the new story already begun.

3

Goldthorn Park via the Dudley Road

Kuli Kohli

In suburbia the trees shake hands, arching over
the streets of Goldthorn, leafy mowed lawns
where roses, lavender, mock orange scent the air.

Frustrated fumes of early morning traffic,
taken in standing at the bus shelter waiting,
while the locals are on the scheduled school run.

Watch where you step though, dodge street litter,
the pong of dog, fox, rat, badger and bird droppings,
the rain washing it away every now and again.

Two minutes down the road, a giant Aldi stands
at the Fighting Cocks junction. Shopper's paradise,
tantalizing smells where Europe meets the globe.

K. Kohli (✉)
Wolverhampton, UK

Dudley Road's exotic aromas diffuse and entice-
masala dosa, fish and chips, grilled meats, sweet
warm scribbles of saffron *jalebis* to satisfy appetites.

A welcoming of calming sandalwood incense,
eastern flavours the Blakenhall Shopping Precinct
mouth watering whiffs of exotic fruits and herbs.

The *Gurdwara's* golden dome greets the community
in supplies of flour, grain, expressions of appreciation,
free fresh food in the *langar* hall - *daal, roti*, spiced *chai*.

Returning after work is like arriving home to the Punjab -
strong fragrances of fried onions, garlic, ginger, chili,
turmeric, garam masala, coriander in easterly breeze.

Glossary

Dosa—Indian savory pancakes made from rice batter
Jalebis—Indian sticky sweets (street food)
Gurdwara—Sikh place of worship
Langar—Free Kitchen
Daal, Roti, Chai—Lentils, Chapatti, Tea

4

The Future Is Elsewhere: Contemporary Black Country Writing

Paul McDonald

In 2002 I published a monograph on the fiction of the Black Country, a Midlands region that began to develop a distinct identity in the nineteenth century. *Fiction from the Furnace: A Hundred Years of Black Country Writing* addresses eight authors publishing between the 1870s and the 1970s: David Christie Murray (1847–1907), Helen Thorneycroft Fowler (1860–1929), Francis Brett Young (1884–1954), George Woden (1884–1979), Henry Treece (1911–1966), Maurice Wiggin (1912–1986), John Petty (1919–1973), and Archie Hill (1928–1986). Among other things, I argue that their work betrays a marked ambivalence towards the region itself: typically it presents a conflict between the rural and industrial, with the former seen as a benign antidote to the latter. Above all, the Black Country signifies negatively: the term itself suggests a tainted region, conjuring images of a blackened country and corrupted nature—a place where industry is a pernicious encroachment on a pastoral idyll. David Christie Murray's idea of the Black Country as

P. McDonald (✉)
University of Wolverhampton, Wolverhampton, UK

S. Groes et al. (eds.), *Smell, Memory, and Literature in the Black Country,*
https://doi.org/10.1007/978-3-030-57212-9_4

a 'sore on a body otherwise healthy',[1] for instance, is reiterated in various ways throughout the region's writing.

This notion extends beyond aesthetics to morality: in Murray, as elsewhere, Black Country industry is seen to have created unethical social structures, conducive only to exploitation and oppression. Any potential for happiness tends to be associated with escape, whether back into nature, as in Treece's *The Rebels* (1953), or to a heavenly paradise, as in Fowler's *The Farringdons* (1900). Where escape isn't possible, the consequences are dire, as witnessed even in the lives of Black Country authors themselves: see, for instance, John Petty's psychosis in his autobiography, *The Face* (1972), or Archie Hill's alcoholism in his memoirs, *A Cage of Shadows* (1973) and *An Empty Glass* (1984). *Fiction from the Furnace* explores writing of the industrial Black Country, then, a region that has suffered a long history of social stigmatisation, reflecting attitudes expressed in the traditional Black Country rhyme with which I open my monograph:

> When Satan stood on Brierley Hill
> and far around him gazed,
> He said, 'I never more shall feel
> at Hell's fierce flames amazed'.
> He staggered on to Dudley Woodside
> And there he laid him down and died.[2]

The modern, deindustrialised Black Country is a different kind of place, of course: manufacturing has largely given way to service industries, which have had a significant effect on working life and urban landscapes. Also the region has witnessed various attempts to reclaim its image, as Esther Asprey writes:

> Today the term 'Black Country' has enjoyed a resurgence as an area in heavy postindustrial decline seeks to move forward and attract business and tourism to the area. What was once a stigmatised label for some is now actively employed by Borough Councils including Sandwell, Dudley and Wolverhampton, by Government agencies, and crucially, residents themselves, in constructing a sense of region and of language.[3]

The aim of this essay, however, is to show that any 'resurgence', or attempts to destigmatise the region, are not reflected in the region's literary fiction: the negative view that informs industrial writing persists in the fiction of the deindustrialised Black Country. I will show the various forms this takes in the work of six of the most notable contemporary Black Country fiction writers: Joel Lane, Kerry Hadley-Pryce, Meera Syal, Sathnam Sangera, Anthony Cartwright, and Catherine O'Flynn.

The Weird Black Country: Joel Lane and Kerry Hadley-Pryce

The novelist, poet, critic, and short story writer, Joel Lane, set much of his work in the region, particularly his highly regarded weird tales, many of which were collected following his premature death in 2013. His story, 'Those Who Remember', for instance, is set in Oldbury and told from the point of view of a mysterious young man, visiting the town after a period away:

> Night had fallen when I reached Oldbury. The best time for coming home: when the new developments fade into the background and the past becomes real again. Over the years I've seen expressways carve up the landscape and titanic, jerry-built tower blocks loom above the familiar terraces. The town was boxed in by industrial estates built on the sites of old factories. Instead of real things like steel and brick, the new businesses manufactured 'office space' and 'electronics'. Only the night could make me feel at home.[4]

Everything seems to have changed in Oldbury for this unnamed visitor-narrator, but as we read on we learn that nothing really has. He is himself an example of the past made 'real again'—the ghost of gay man murdered years ago, who now haunts his hometown, a place where he suffered at the hands of his homophobic peers. The latter includes Dean, whose house he now visits. Dean is a drug addict, and the visitor insists on helping him go cold turkey, then commands him to murder two of his friends, Wayne and Richard, who were among those who tormented him in his youth. Dean fails to murder them, and we learn that this is a regular ritual, with the deceased visitor reappearing every few years to make the same demand. We learn too that Dean is a repressed homosexual who once had sex with the visitor on a camping trip, but then murdered him, presumably out of guilt. The ritual hauntings look like the return of the repressed for Dean, then, and always conclude in an identical way: with the narrator inviting Dean to stab him between the shoulder blades. This ritual takes place, significantly, in a derelict house, a symbol of the blighted Black Country: inside this relic of the past, Dean and his visitor re-enact their murderous history, implying stasis rather than change; in other words, while the landscape may alter superficially, the dark heart of the region, with its violence and bigotry, beats on.

In his criticism, Joel Lane distinguished between what he termed 'existential horror' and 'ontological horror'. While the former can be understood in human terms, the latter starts from the assumption that, 'humans cannot use their own nature as a key to the reality that surrounds them'.[5] In his own work, Lane brings together these two traditions. Thus we can rationalise the appearance of the avenging figure in 'Those Who Remember', and explain it in Freudian terms, but some elements point to forces beyond human understanding. This is particularly so with the link between the visitor's revenge and the regional landscape, particularly the erosion of the things that he feels give life meaning: the 'steel and brick' that's now replaced by the simulations of 'the new businesses'. There's an implied connection between Oldbury's inability to improve, and the mistakes of the past that persist in the present: Dean is still a drug addict, still in denial about his sexuality, and still content to re-enact his symbolic ritual whenever the visitor appears in his life. As the narrator tells us, 'those who forget the past are condemned to repeat it. And those who remember do it anyway'.[6] There's no possibility of escape or progress here, then, and no easy way to rationalise the weird world that Lane constructs. As in many Lane stories, the final words suggest that any change will only be for the worse: 'Nothing lasts forever, and there's no eternal. Everything falls apart in the end'.[7]

For Lane, the changing Black Country landscape becomes symbolic of the inevitability of decline: while Oldbury has altered superficially, the mindset of the people has not, and their fate is inescapable. It implies an entropy that cannot be fathomed, and which precludes human intervention; moreover, this decline is manifest in the fabric of the landscape itself: a material and moral decay that is seemingly in tandem.

Lane's reading of the human condition is pessimistic, and the urban landscapes of the post-industrial Midlands offer the perfect context in which to explore this. He was a political writer in many ways, appalled by the impact of Thatcherism on the region, but the origins of evil run to deeper, largely unfathomable realms. While his heroes desperately seek explanations, they are rarely forthcoming. This is particularly so with the detective-hero of the stories in his 2014 collection, *Where Furnaces Burn*. In 'My Stone Desire', for instance, Lane's narrator does his police training in Wolverhampton, becoming a policeman because, in police work, 'there was no room for the unknown'[8]; his experiences soon teach otherwise, however, and evil appears to exist for unknowable reasons. While the Black Country provides the hero with some amusements—via live music venues and opportunities for socialising—these are meagre and transient. He and his girlfriend, Kath, are soon separated, despite having a child together: there's a degree of inevitability about this linked to the fact that she hails from what he terms, 'the estranged heart of the Black Country', and speaks 'the Tipton dialect, which no one outside the town can understand'.[9] His Black Country girlfriend is a mystery, just like the crimes he is employed to solve. When people begin disappearing in Wolverhampton, he is assigned to investigate. He is 'frustrated by the lack of answers', until one night he wanders down by a mouldy railway bridge to find that, the 'structure of the bridge was made up of tightly packed, naked human bodies, twisted together in the warmth of slow decay'. Weirder still is his realisation that, 'they hadn't been killed and left there. They'd gone there of their own accord'.[10] The denizens of Lane's Black Country find a bizarre community in death—one that they were presumably unable to find in life. His alienated Black Country folk literally merge with the fabric of the railway bridge, becoming part of the structure that, ironically, bears the track that might have carried them somewhere better—a world with more potential than his bleak, inexplicably warped Black Country. That they choose death instead of escape suggests that there is, in fact, no escape: that the Black Country is symbolic of a greater, ubiquitous evil, in the face of which Lane's detective is left helpless and shaking.

The idea of the Black Country as an inexplicably malign environment is taken up again in the noir fiction of Kerry Hadley-Pryce. Her debut novel, *The Black Country* (2015), presents a world that is as dark and degenerate as Lane's. It tells the story of Maddie and Harry, whose destructive relationship is played out in a toxic environment. Each has been unfaithful to the other: Maddie having secretly conceived a child outside the marriage; Harry, who ironically teaches moral philosophy, having seduced a fourteen-year-old schoolgirl. While attending a college reunion at Oakhall Manor, Maddie has drunken sex with a man, Jonathan, only to accidentally run him over on the journey home. Maddie and Harry leave him for dead, blaming each other.

The Black Country is a potent signifier in the story, and portentous from the beginning: on the morning of the accident, for instance, we're told that Maddie feels 'that awkward kind of Black Country darkness [...] as if she'd suddenly fallen into freezing water, or someone had walked over her grave'.[11] As in many Black Country novels before it, this one depicts the urban and the rural as a binary opposition, privileging the latter over the former. Thus on their journey out of the Black Country towards Oakhall Manor, Maddie and Harry drive away from the 'gritty Midlands toward the intermittent promise of the Worcestershire hills'; as they move towards the 'promise' of the rural, they are, we're told, 'leaving behind that toxic looking Black Country landscape'.[12] It's on the road back to the 'toxic' Black Country that the accident happens, and, following the event, returning home feels like 'driving right into Hell'.[13] Here, then, we have the urban/rural dichotomy presented in biblical terms, where an urban 'Hell' is set against a rural 'paradise', the opposing poles of a black/country binary. The relationship between the Black Country and darkness is reinforced later when Maddie hits herself in the face with a wooden hairbrush. She bloodies herself, we're told, like 'an angry, hurt, lovely vampire', and the impulse is equated with 'the dark, Black Country in her'.[14] Whether this amounts to a form of penance, or irrational self-harm, it appears that the spirit of the Black Country is both violent and perverse.

The atmosphere of mystery and contingency is augmented by the fact that the story is told by an absent character-narrator whose identity is concealed until the end. The narrator conveys events as if they've been related to him second hand by Maddie and Harry, who, it turns out, he is holding captive. The narrator qualifies everything he says with phrases like 'would have said' and 'apparently said', underscoring his subjectivity. This has the effect of distancing us from the action, but also of creating the impression of an unstable, unknowable world. The narrator is further revealed as the father of Maddie's child, Faith, who he also holds captive, and who is revealed as the schoolgirl that Harry seduced. Significantly, the evil driving the narrator is strongly linked to the region. We're told, for instance, that he lives in Clent, a place which resembles 'a couple of wet rags dumped on the horizon amongst the thin plumes of Black Country smoke', and which he refers to specifically as Hell: 'I think I am dead, and this is Hell'.[15] Unlike with Lane, there is no obvious supernatural element here, and Maddie and Harry are partly victims of their own moral frailty, and ultimately of a madman. However, the clear links made between moral corruption and the Black Country complicates this, adding elements that transcend the rational world, suggesting common ground with Lane. As the latter once wrote:

> there is a grain of ontological horror within the noir strand of crime fiction - it may purely be metaphorical, but it's there. Noir fiction explores the experience of dehumanisation, loss of identity, loss of moral centre. It is therefore rich in images of the nonhuman.[16]

The Black Country falls into the genre of noir fiction in this sense. Both Hadley-Pryce and Lane convey a darkness that cannot easily be rationalised—it is a dehumanising Black Country that lacks a moral centre, where characters flounder for reasons that, despite Lane's often overt political references, aren't obvious. The area just seems to complement their tales of suffering and moral decay. However, other writers find more explicit reasons for their negative portrayals of the region, as will be seen.

Being Brown in the Black Country: Meera Syal and Sathnam Sanghera

By far the most popular Black Country-based stories of the past three decades have come from two of the region's British Asian writers, Meera Syal and Sathnam Sanghra, for whom representations of the region are linked to issues of race and identity.

Meera Syal's *Anita and Me* (1997) is a coming of age novel, narrated by Meena Kumar, a second generation Punjabi girl living in 60s Tollington, a fictional version of the author's home town, Essington. Tollington—like 60s Essington—is an isolated town with a distinctly rural and parochial feel. Its 'cosy village idyll'[17] is threatened by plans to build a new motorway extension, something that actually happened to Essington with the construction of the M54; so events occur against a background of impending change, reflecting a real historical moment. The young Meena rebels against the role she's expected to play at home as a 'good' Indian girl, as represented by her cousins, Pinky and Baby, 'whose […] girlish modesty gave me the urge to roll naked in the pigsties shouting obscenities'.[18] Meena finds the antidote to them in the earthy, Black Country wench, Anita Rutter: a coarse, rambunctious product of a dysfunctional family, and the antithesis of Pinky and Baby. However, Meena is caught uncomfortably between identities, and cultures:

> I knew I was a freak of some kind, too mouthy, clumsy and scabby to be a real Indian girl, too Indian to be a real Tollington wench, but living in the grey area between all categories.[19]

Her conflict is expressed linguistically too, as clash between Punjabi, Black Country dialect, and standard English. Meena's ethnic heritage is represented by Punjabi, a language her elders speak but she cannot; her father wants her to learn, but she associates it with problems, 'a sign that something was […] probably bad news' (25). The other discourse at Meena's disposal, apart from standard English, is the Black Country dialect. She uses this to express solidarity with Anita, impressing her with her 'authentic Yard accent' (122). Just as Punjabi is associated with trouble, so the Black Country dialect also causes problems, creating friction within her family. When she uses dialect with her father, for instance, we're told that 'Papa winced at the slang which I used deliberately' (148). Thus Meena is caught between cultures *and* between modes of expression.

Ultimately the language that Meena embraces is neither Punjabi nor Black Country dialect, but standard English—the primary discourse of the novel. Meena narrates her story in the first person, from a mature perspective: it is the voice of an educated English speaker, and any departures from the standard form—be they Black Country dialect or Punjabi—are mediated by the adult Meena, and mostly employed for satirical purposes. At the end of the story Meena is going to grammar school, and her Aunt gives her a leaving present of a pen: it's a symbolic gift, and the first thing she does with it is a symbolic act—she writes a goodbye note to Anita. Up till this point Meena's exchanges with Anita have been in dialect, but her final communication is in written, standard English—the discourse representing her future and her freedom. It implies that it's Meena's education that will provide an alternative both to the parochialism of Anita's world, and the conformity of Pinky and Baby.

The novel suggests that Meena's future lies beyond *both* working-class Black Country society *and* Hindu culture, and this point is made in other ways too. When Meena returns to Tollington after her long stay in hospital, for instance, a new road has been opened linking Tollington to the world beyond: she is struck by the fact that the 'cornfields were the only stretch of land separating us from the 'townies'.[20] But Meena realises that such change is inevitable, and, above all, necessary. In the closing pages it is stasis, rather than change that Meena criticises. She does so initially with reference Anita's fascist friends: with their 'denim and leather and braces and lace-up Doctor Martens, heads shorn like summer sheep [...] a colourless, humourless island in this sea of change'.[21] Thus, for Meena, it's the stupid people and the bigots who cannot accept change. By the end of the novel she is able to put Anita and her friends into perspective, realising that she isn't defined by them or the meagre environment of Tollington. However, she isn't defined solely by her Punjabi heritage either. At the close Meena also rejects the potential judgements of her family, telling us that: 'I now knew that I was not a bad girl'. She rejects both the parochialism and small mindedness of Tollington teenagers like Anita, *and* the constraints of straight-laced Indian culture. This is what frees her from her psychological snare, made explicit when she tells us she's no longer, 'a mixed up girl [...] with no name or place [...] there was nothing stopping me simply moving forward and claiming each resting place as my home' (303). Moving forward means becoming a citizen of the world beyond Tollington, and it's fitting that the final image of the town is as a place no longer cut off from the rest of the world:

> I saw that Tollington had lost its edges and boundaries, that the motorway bled into another road and another and the Barlett estate had swallowed up the last cornfield and that my village was indistinguishable from the suburban mass that had once surrounded it and had finally swallowed it whole. It was time to let go and I floated back into my body which, for the first time ever, fitted me to perfection and was all mine. (326)

It's only when the village is seen as part of a whole that Meena *herself* becomes whole. The message is clear—the answer to her problems lies with embracing the broader community, not with social isolation or cultural introspection. *Anita and Me* presents the Black Country as something Meena must outgrow, then, and this is mirrored in the novel by the limitations of Hindu culture, which she must also leave behind. They are both targets of Syals' satire, and Meena can only feel whole, and free, once she's jettisoned both; this means education and social integration, represented by the grammar school and the motorway respectively: two routes away from the region for Meena.

The cultural tensions that create the comedy in Syal also feature heavily in the work of Wolverhampton born, Sathnam Sanghera. He first came to national attention with *If You Don't Know Me by Now* (2008)— later retitled, *Boy with a Topknot*—where he presents his experiences of growing up Sikh in the Black Country during the 80s and 90s. It deals with the problems he has reconciling his ethnic and regional heritage with the culturally sophisticated life he comes to lead as an adult in London, and offers a touching account of his family's struggle to cope with his father's schizophrenia. It's this that forces Sanghera back to the

Black Country, providing the catalyst for the memoir. Consider this account of his return to Wolverhampton by road:

> after the hills and spires on the horizon began to be replaced with shabby factories and the shimmering tops of newly built gurdwaras, I once again found myself in Wolverhampton, the arse of the Black Country, in itself the bumrack of the West Midlands, in itself the backside of Great Britain.[22]

Sanghera's disparaging description is meant to ratchet up the comic tone, of course, in keeping with the idea that ugly places are funnier than beautiful places. Returning to the Black Country from the comparative glamour and sophistication of London is clearly going to be a hilarious ordeal for him: he later spends time parodying the Black Country accent, expressing astonishment that Wolverhampton should have a Tourist Information Centre, and generally presenting the region as provincial and unpleasant. He associates it with the past, like his Sikh heritage: he satirises both in equal measure, deeming them comically unsophisticated, backward-looking, and meagre. That they both become the butt of Sanghera's humour suggests an important parallel between the two in the author's mind, implicit in his linking of 'shabby factories' and 'shimmering gurdwaras' in the quote above. Like Syal's narrator, the mature Sanghera feels he has outgrown both.

The key symbol of his Sikh identity is his topknot, and he takes the momentous decision to have this cut off while studying at Wolverhampton Grammar School: it's noteworthy that he discards this, not as is traditional, in running water, but in a Wolverhampton canal: 'wrongly assuming that the water flowed. Most likely, my disembodied plait is still languishing at the bottom of Broad Street locks'.[23] We can't help feeling how appropriate this error is, allowing him to consign his religion—and its hypocrisies and comic superstitions—to the stagnant waters of the 'arse of the Black Country'. The parallel between the two is further reinforced at the end of the book when Sanghera invites his mother to London and opens his heart about his desire to marry for love. After arriving at some kind of understanding, we're told that 'when I went home with Mum to Wolverhampton [...] we immediately returned to our usual bickering'.[24] Thus Wolverhampton is associated with the bickering past, and the constraints that his mother's religious fervour imposes.

As several critics have noted, positive change for Sanghera is linked with assimilation, and the position he has attained among the cultural elite: in other words, it lies in cultivated London rather than provincial Prosser Street. Kavita Bhanot, for instance, argues that *Topknot* becomes a kind of 'misery memoir' where the hero is redeemed by his transition from economic and cultural impoverishment to a life of wealth and social sophistication:

> The 'misery' of the misery memoir is constituted primarily by the fact of 'Asianness', the author having been born into a working-class South Asian and Sikh family. At the heart of both genres is the assumption of a normative white and middle-class gaze. From that location, and for that readership, the writer shares his/her difficult and yet ultimately triumphant journey.[25]

This triumphant journey for Sanghera, as with Syal, is a journey away from both 'Asianness' and the Black Country.

Sanghera's debut novel, *Marriage Material* (2014), constructs a similar cultural conflict in the form of a hero, Arjan Banger, who is forced to return to Wolverhampton following his father's death. Arjan has been working in London as a graphic designer, engaged to a white woman, Freya. He is required to help his mother run the family newsagent following the bereavement, and, like Sanghera in *Topknot*, he is torn between this and his former life. Alongside this story, which takes place during the summer of 2011, is the story of his parents and grandparents' struggles to establish themselves as immigrants in the Black Country of the late 60s. The racial tensions of the 60s, fuelled by Wolverhampton MP Enoch Powell's notorious 'Rivers of Blood' speech, seem to parallel the social unease of 2011, the summer which saw rioting on the streets of Wolverhampton. The implication is that, despite surface differences, nothing much has changed in the Black Country, as Arjan himself notes following a night of rioting:

Intellectually, I appreciated that my community and my home town, not least my own life, stood as a testament to the fact that Enoch Powell was not right. But the longer I spent in the shop, the harder it became to hold on to this thesis. In my heart of hearts, I couldn't forget that the only Asians on the streets of Wolverhampton that night were shop owners, or people trying to protect the shop owners. All the looters I'd seen were black and white. And once I had accepted this, started seeing the world in monochrome, embraced casual racism, I felt liberated.[26]

Arjan's return to the Black Country undermines his liberal education, and the political correctness central to his civilised values: he is in danger of becoming a Black Country bigot!

As with *Topknot*, there is also a clear parallel drawn between Black Country parochialism and the shortcomings of Sikh culture. The racism of the former, for instance, has its equivalent in the caste system of the latter, something which proves key to the plot when it becomes evident that Arjan's father was murdered for belonging to an inferior caste. Where in his 'misery memoir', Sanghera's own 'misery' lies at the heart of the narrative, it's Arjan's aunty, Surinder, who is made miserable in *Marriage Material*, both by her region and her religion. Frustrated at the constraints imposed on her by tradition, and fearing an arranged marriage, she flees Wolverhampton with a salesman, James O'Connor, who woos her, significantly, 'not in a Black Country drawl, but in a sing-song Irish lilt'.[27] While the marriage is a disaster, she goes on to become a successful business woman, only returning to Wolverhampton later in life to help Arjan and his mother, Kamaljit, with their failing newsagents. Kamaljit's death ultimately frees Arjan and his aunt from their responsibilities in Wolverhampton, effectively facilitating the novel's happy ending: Arjan marries his formerly estranged fiancée, Freya, in a modern Sikh wedding ceremony, and the pair move back to London, along with Surinder. At the close, Arjan contemplates opening an art gallery, while Surinder might open a cafe: the fact that we are told that it 'would have to be one of the poncy kinds that wouldn't last a minute in Blaken-fields' underscores the assumptions and values that underpin the novel.[28] Success for highfliers like Arjan and his aunt can only be achieved *outside* the region, and while Arjan's Sikh wedding offers a gesture of respect for his heritage, his decision to marry Freya and return to London confirms that his values and ambitions remain largely unchanged.

With both Syal and Sanghera, we see an assimilationist message that equates Notions of Black Country parochialism with ethnic and religious naivety: while region and ethnic heritage are occasionally treated with nostalgia and affection, progress means assimilation into a broader culture via education, and geographical relocation.

The Decline of Industry: Anthony Cartwright and Catherine O'Flynn

Something that interests Sanghera in *Marriage Material* is the effects of the economy on the Black Country, particularly through the 1980s, when the 'collapse of traditional industry had left Wolverhampton with one of the highest rates of long term unemployment in Britain'.[29] The shift to a retail-based economy has had huge implications, with the construction of retail parks 'located, catastrophically, just outside the ring road, ensuring that there was no need for residents to go anywhere near the town centre'.[30] As a consequence, the Wolverhampton that Sanghera describes is 'named the worst [city] in the country yet again for empty shops',[31] and not even the '£22.5 million bus station, the most ambitious infrastructure project the city had seen in years'[32] can redeem it: we're told that, '[a]s with so many Wolverhampton developments, it didn't look quite finished [...] the city being most at its ease when it resembles a building site'.[33] This is the deindustrialised Black Country, the landscape and economy that interests Anthony Cartwright and Catherine O'Flynn.

Anthony Cartwright's first published story, 'Leaf Patterns', appeared in the early 2000s, and contains many of the themes of his later fiction: the decline of Black Country industry, the importance of family, and football. Set in the early 1990s Dudley, it opens with a young man, Luke, scoring a goal for his school team. He is watched from the side-lines by a girl he likes, Becky, who he hopes is also interested in him. After the game he walks her to her bus stop, but when he thinks she's about to declare her feelings for him, she reveals that she actually likes his friend Nicky, and wants Luke to put in a good word for her:

Look, yer know how Nicky ay gooin out wi nobody at the minute and
wi yow bein such good mates wi him I wondered if he ud goo out wi me,
like.
All in a rush, in one breath
Oh, wi Nicky, right. He tried not to show anything in his voice.[34]

It's a story of maturation in which the hero learns that the world isn't fair:
while Luke is a sensitive and caring character, Nicky is presented as selfish
and conceited, and yet it's him who gets the girl. What distinguishes the
story is the impressive way the author grounds Luke's experience in its
regional setting. Cartwright employs precise location indicators like St
James's Road and Dudley Bus station, a connection to place which is
reinforced by the use of dialect, for which Cartwright has an impeccable
ear. Unlike in the satirical novels of Syal and Sanghera, dialect is not
used for comic effect here; rather it is employed to reinforce our sense of
the characters' common predicament, and the idea of a Black Country
community.

Luke wants to hold on to the feeling he had after scoring his goal,
when everything was perfect for a moment, and he even considers saving
a leaf he sees stuck to his football sock as a souvenir. The fact that the
story takes place in autumn, however, suggests that such ambitions are
doomed: the leaf, like all leaves, will fall away, and the story is partly
about the inevitability of change. This idea is also linked to the region:
as Luke walks home after leaving Becky, we're told that: 'He walked
past the steps that used to lead up to the factory, packed with rubbish
and brambles'.[35] In this way Cartwright establishes a subtle connection
between his hero's inability to retain happiness, and the decline of his
hometown, with its abandoned, rubbish strewn factories. Luke's disillusionment parallels the region's decline, and neither he, nor his home
town, has any choice but to cope with the harsh reality of change. The
compensations for Luke, as in Cartwright's later fiction, are football, and
the community itself, particularly his own family:

He walked the long way home after that. It would be OK [...] He
thought about the way he was going to describe his goal to his dad,
pictured sitting at the kitchen table, it was bacon and eggs tonight [...]
And it was Littlewood's Cup night. Midweek Sports Special would be on

and he could sit up late watching it with a cup of tea and cheese on toast
[...] And his goal. He could think about his goal [...] The way the ball
almost stopped completely before he hit it. He walked up the hill trying
to get that feeling, trying to get that feeling back.[36]

The references to the Littlewood's Cup and Midweek Sports Special,
together with the story's other social references, specific locations, and
use of dialect, all help ground 'Leaf Patterns' in a working-class culture
that, as with Luke's goal, offer only transient comfort: in time all will
be consigned to the irretrievable past, like the rubbish strewn factory,
remnant of the town's lost industry.

Such changes are Cartwright's principal theme in his debut novel, *The
Afterglow* (2004), where Luke appears again, now working in a meatpacking factory, ironically named Paradise Meatpacking. The loss of
the industry that left a generation unemployed in the Black Country,
including Luke's own father, is paralleled here by the theme of bereavement: the loss of Luke's brother, Adam, who was killed by a truck as
a small boy. The characters struggle to come to terms with both, and
Luke in particular is plagued by the feeling that he was to blame for his
brother's death. Luke fantasises about becoming a success, leaving the
Black Country to return in the future as a hero, but, realising that this
is a hollow dream, he considers himself a failure in life. However, as Phil
O'Brien suggests, he is more a victim of the effects of deindustrialisation
on the region, than of any personal shortcomings.[37] There are precious
few opportunities for people like Luke, beyond Paradise Meatpacking:
deindustrialisation has created a fractured and meagre Black Country, as
his father understands:

> Iss a crime, he thought to himself, what happened was a crime. Yow tek
> these thousands o blokes, working, mekkin summat, for God's sake, livin
> theer lives, and the families they had, and the communities arahnd em.
> Not just the Round Oak, loads o plaeces. An yer just crush it. Just like
> tha. An yow expect everythin to goo on as normal afterwards. Well, things
> doh work like tha.[38]

The characters are blighted by their sociocultural circumstances: by the
Black Country, and the vicissitudes of the economic system that once

sustained it. Here, and in Cartwright's fiction generally, success is associated with a life beyond the region: for Luke this is 'overseas somewhere, fighting a war, or making his fortune'[39]; for others it is the traditional routes out of working-class life, like football, which features extensively in later novels such as *Heartland* and *Iron Towns* (2016); likewise, a return to the Black Country tends to be associated with failure, as is the case with the central characters in the latter novel who, after minor successes beyond the region, are returned to the place that 'leans in on itself, subsides', and where, 'walls fall slowly and roofs sag, a slow-motion catastrophe ... a long slow drift into silence'.[40]

The social impact of late twentieth-century government policy on the Black Country is also explored in Catherine O'Flynn's 2007 novel, *What Was Lost*. At the heart of this is Green Oaks Shopping Centre, which is clearly modelled on the Merry Hill Centre, constructed just outside Dudley in the 1980s. The plot concerns the disappearance of Kate Meaney, who goes missing aged 10 in 1984, only to seemingly reappear on a Green Oaks CCTV camera twenty years later. The security guard who spots her, Kurt, and a sympathetic Green Oaks employee, Lisa, work together to untangle the mystery of Kate's disappearance. As in *The Afterglow*, the idea of loss is twofold, referring both to the death of a child, and the consequences of industrial decline. Green Oaks was built on the site of the factory that employed Kurt's father, for instance, and the loss of that job had an unmanning effect on him, and a negative impact on the family generally:

> Kurt realised that his secret places and all his silent industrial playgrounds were going. He had watched the scaffolding go up, and now come down again, for the new shopping centre opening a few hundred yards away. Already his father had forbidden any of the family to visit Green Oaks. The shopping centre was built on the site of his old factory, and Kurt Sr clearly saw it as an insult to the whole area, a place where women would work and women would shop and nothing would be made of any value.[41]

The cost of Green Oaks is both social and psychological: it replaced the sites of manufacture that gave work to people like Kurt Sr, and undermined the traditional High Street, which now looks on with its 'reproachful boarded up doorways filled with fast-food debris and leaves'.[42] Green Oaks itself is seen as an insubstantial, two dimensional world offering mere simulations of what it replaced: a veneer concealing a dark, empty interior:

> the parallel unseen universe of the service corridors. Mile upon mile of pipes, wires, ventilator shafts, fuse cupboards, security barriers, fire hoses. Like an illuminated cave network, narrow passages would abruptly bloom into cavernous loading bays and other lanes would lead nowhere. Everything glowed grey, everything smelled of hot dust.[43]

This is the murky unconscious of Green Oaks, where, as it turns out, Kate Meaney's corpse has lain for twenty years. For consumers, meanwhile, Green Oaks offers only false promises of satisfaction. For instance, the novel includes passages from several anonymous characters, all of whom are associated with Green Oaks in various ways: a mystery shopper, a glue sniffing teenager, and several faceless customers engaged in pointless shopping:

> We haven't found anything we want to buy today. We're going in all the right shops but nothing's really grabbing us. It's raining outside, though, so what else would we be doing? Sitting at home staring at each other. Going up the walls on Sunday afternoon, that's what we used to do. Thank God for Sunday trading.[44]

The irony of the final line is telling, of course, hinting at the false values this new world has created. While the speaker praises Green Oaks, he simultaneously acknowledges his inability to satiate his needs there. Like all of the central characters, these peripheral, anonymous people are all lost in one way or another, and the answer to their alienation, if there is one, is not to be found in the false promise of consumer culture. Throughout the story, Lisa has a cynical and ironic perspective on both consumer culture and the dream of social advancement: she leaves her boyfriend, Ed, for instance, partly because he wants to get a mortgage on new build accommodation near the Green Oaks development. Where Ed blindly embraces the empty life that Green Oaks offers, Lisa has more discernment, and her irony is a form of inoculation against the spurious values of the modern Black Country. The novel's ending sees Kurt and Lisa about to begin a romantic relationship: while they have both lived unfulfilled lives in the region, it's suggested that they may find solace in each other. We can read this as a symbolic union of like-minded people, suggesting that a positive future depends on those who don't 'buy in' to the modern Black Country, either literally or emotionally.

Conclusion

Despite the attempts to reinvent itself noted at the outset, the region continues to have negative connotations in contemporary literary fiction. For Cartwright and O'Flynn, this is linked directly to the social consequences of deindustrialisation: the decline in manufacturing and the rise of service industries in a region founded on industry is dehumanising and alienating; it is seen as a blighted region, linked literally and metaphorically to loss, death, and disillusionment.

In Syal and Sanghera, the Black Country is parochial and limiting, implicitly equated with the obligations and constraints of ethnic heritage; it is seen as a place to escape, associated with a culture that should be rejected in the process of education, and assimilation into more prestigious social strata. But at least there is a possibility of escape for their heroes, which isn't the case in the Black Country of Lane and Hadley-Pryce: here characters seem oddly resigned to their misery, and a world that's inherently and inexplicably lacking. It is one that returns us to the traditional Black Country rhyme with which I began this paper, and the image of the place where the 'Devil laid him down and died'. For the Devil, and for the contemporary Black Country writers addressed here, the future still seems to be elsewhere.

Notes

1. Paul McDonald, *Fiction from the Furnace: A Hundred Years of Black Country Writing* (Sheffield: Sheffield Hallam University Press, 2002), 19.
2. Quoted in Jon Raven, *Stories, Customs, superstition, Tales, Legends and Folklore in the Black Country and Staffordshire* (Wolverhampton: Broadside, 1986), 23.
3. Esther Asprey, 'Black Country Dialect Literature and What It Can Tell Us About Black Country dialect', in *Dialect Writing and the North of England*, edited by Patrick Honeybone and Warren Maguire (Edinburgh: Edinburgh University Press, Forthcoming), 27–45; 27.
4. Joel Lane, 'Those Who Remember', in *Scar City* (London: Eibonvale Press, 2015), 17–27; 17.
5. Joel Lane, 'This Spectacular Darkness', in *This Spectacular Darkness*, edited by Mark Valentine and John Howard (Carlton, Leyburn: Tartarus Press, 2016), 1–15; 3–4.
6. Lane, Remember, 20.
7. Lane, Remember, 25.
8. Joel Lane, 'My Stone Desire', in *Where Furnaces Burn* (Hornsea: Drugstore Indiana Press, 2014), 3–9; 3.
9. Lane, Stone Desire, 4.
10. Lane, Stone Desire, 7.
11. Kerry Hadley-Pryce, *The Black Country* (Cromer: Salt, 2015), 13.
12. Hadley-Pryce, 18.
13. Hadley-Pryce, 33.
14. Hadley-Pryce, 60.
15. Hadley-Pryce, 157, 162.
16. Lane, Spectacular Darkness, 6.
17. Meera Syal, *Anita and Me* (London: Flamingo, 1997), 142.
18. Syal, *Anita*, 148.
19. Syal, *Anita*, 149–150.
20. Syal, *Anita*, 299.
21. Syal, *Anita*, 299.
22. Sathnam Sanghera, *If You Don't Know Me by Now: A Memoir of Love Secrets and Lies in Wolverhampton* (London: Viking, 2008), 51.

23. Sanghera, *If You Don't Know*, 250.
24. Sanghera, *If You Don't Know*, 316–317.
25. Kavita Bhanot, 'Reading the Whiteness of British Asian Literature: A Reading of Sathnam Sanghera's *The Boy with the Topknot: A Memoir of Love, Secrets and Lies in Wolverhampton*', *The Journal of Commonwealth Literature* (2 April 2018). https://journals.sagepub.com/doi/10.1177/002 1989418759741.
26. Sathnam Sanghera, *Marriage Material* (London: Windmill Books, 2014), 116.
27. Sanghera, *Marriage*, 70.
28. Sanghera, *Marriage*, 302.
29. Sanghera, *Marriage*, 264.
30. Sanghera, *Marriage*, 264.
31. Sanghera, *Marriage*, 281.
32. Sanghera, *Marriage*, 212.
33. Sanghera, *Marriage*, 212.
34. Anthony Cartwright, 'Leaf Patterns', *Raw Edge*, no. 17 (Autumn/Winter 2003/4): 7, iii.
35. Cartwright, 'Leaf Patterns', 7, iv.
36. Cartwright, 'Leaf Patterns', 7, iv.
37. Phil O'Brien, 'The Deindustrial Novel: Twenty First Century British Fiction and the Working Class', in *Working-Class Writing: Theory and Practice*, edited by Ben Clarke and Nick Hubble (London: Palgrave Macmillan, 2018), 229–246; 236.
38. Anthony Cartwright, *The Afterglow* (Birmingham Tindal Street Press, 2004), 118–119.
39. Cartwright, *The Afterglow*, 104–105.
40. Anthony Cartwright, *Iron Towns* (London: Serpent's Tail, 2016), 81.
41. Catherine O'Flynn, *What Was Lost* (Birmingham: Tindal Street Press, 2007), 106.
42. O'Flynn, *What Was Lost*, 5.
43. O'Flynn, *What Was Lost*, 91.
44. O'Flynn, *What Was Lost*, 151–152.

Works Cited

Asprey, Esther. 'Black Country Dialect Literature and What It Can Tell Us About Black Country Dialect', in *Dialect Writing and the North of England*, edited by Patrick Honeybone and Warren Maguire (Edinburgh: Edinburgh University Press, Forthcoming).

Bhanot, Kavita. 'Reading the Whiteness of British Asian Literature: A Reading of Sathnam Sanghera's *The Boy with the Topknot: A Memoir of Love, Secrets and Lies in Wolverhampton*', *The Journal of Commonwealth Literature* (2 April 2018). https://journals.sagepub.com/doi/10.1177/0021989418759741.

Cartwright, Anthony. 'Leaf Patterns', *Raw Edge*, no. 17 (Autumn/Winter 2003/4): 7, i–iv.

Cartwright, Anthony. *The Afterglow* (Birmingham: Tindal Street Press, 2004).

Cartwright, Anthony. *Iron Towns* (London: Serpent's Tail, 2016).

Hadley-Pryce, Kerry. *The Black Country* (Cromer: Salt, 2015).

Lane, Joel. *Where Furnaces Burn* (Hornsea: Drugstore Indiana Press, 2014).

Lane, Joel. *Scar City* (Eibonvale Press, 2015).

Lane, Joel. *This Spectacular Darkness*, ed. Mark Valentine and John Howard (Carlton, Leyburn: Tartarus Press, 2016), 1–15; 3–4.

McDonald, Paul. *Fiction from the Furnace: A Hundred Years of Black Country Writing* (Sheffield: Sheffield Hallam University Press, 2002).

O'Brien, Phil. 'The Deindustrial Novel: Twenty First Century British Fiction and the Working Class', in *Working-Class Writing: Theory and Practice*, edited by Ben Clarke and Nick Hubble (London: Palgrave Macmillan, 2018), 229–246.

O'Flynn, Catherine. *What Was Lost* (Birmingham: Tindal Street Press, 2007).

Sanghera, Sathnam. *If You Don't Know Me by Now: A Memoir of Love Secrets and Lies in Wolverhampton* (London: Viking, 2008).

Sanghera, Sathnam. *Marriage Material* (London: Windmill Books, 2014).

Syal, Meera. *Anita and Me* (London: Flamingo, 1997).

5

Methyl Methacrylate and the Great Wolverhampton Novel

Anthony Cartwright

The Great Wolverhampton Novel smells of methyl methacrylate, and traffic fumes and ash and iron and blood and rust, of course, but first the methyl methacrylate. Like all great, exhaustive, definitive novels of place, a multi-generational, vast, sprawling epic, the GWN allows for various authorial interjections—I didn't know it was called methyl methacrylate when I used to smell the stuff when washing cars in the works car park at the Fordham Plastics Factory, where my dad worked, and where one or two afternoons a week me and a mate would go to clean cars for two pounds a time (this is the late eighties, early nineties, so felt like good pay if you could get a few lined up). The smell of the yard was that of a very strong nail varnish remover, which overpowered even the ring-road traffic fumes, and which was that of the methyl methacrylate itself. I hated the smell but liked the work, especially when we had a tea break in the Press Shop, where they made cattle drinkers, with the supervisor, Alf, and the lads who worked there. Everyone was a real laugh. If I ever

A. Cartwright (✉)
City, University of London, London, UK

S. Groes et al. (eds.), *Smell, Memory, and Literature in the Black Country*,
https://doi.org/10.1007/978-3-030-57212-9_5

smell nail varnish remover nowadays I think of Wolverhampton. My dad was pleased to tell me that methyl methacrylate was what they'd used to make the windscreen for Concorde, as well as the Asterite sinks and baths in the factory. Apparently, it is sometimes used as the cement in hip and knee replacements today. Fordhams has long gone. The yard I washed the cars in is roughly where the new Next shop is on the St. Johns Retail Park, as it is now called. Supersonic travel replaced by dodgy knees; factories—their smells and everything else—replaced by shopping centres: there's some kind of Black Country story there—Which brings us back to The Great Wolverhampton Novel and how it opens on the aforementioned yard amidst factory ruins on a spring morning in the early 1990s, some time between Fordham's closure and the Retail Park being built. A young man, still in his twenties, but having already lived a hundred lives, called Billy Wright (not that one) lies faces down in the yard, drunk, believing himself to be dead, and smells the distinctive smell in one of the fissures in the uneven concrete. Memories flood back to him of when he worked at Fordhams as a kid just out of school, fetching and carrying in the Press Shop, and he is transported to a happier, safer life when he still had a family around him and he enjoyed a pint at the club on a Friday night and going to the Molinuex on a Saturday, and sometimes later to the speedway, and a game of ten-pin bowling at the old wooden alley in Blakenhall. And so he rises, alive after all, like the smell, taking the smell with him, as well as his own smells of dereliction, to find his lost family on a quest through the streets of Blakenhall and Fighting Cocks and Parkfields.

Cut to a chapter set in a bedroom high above the streets in one of the Blakenhall high-rises where a very old man lies dying. His name is Billy Wright (not that one, either, but in fact the grandad of the young Billy Wright we have already met).

Poised between life and death he has taken to calling things out in recent days that no one can understand, "Cut him open, Harry," he implores, "Fuck it. I'll do it meself." He is surrounded by family and a priest sits at the bedside delivering the last rites. A crucifix and a portrait of Mary hang in the sunlight above the bed, remnants of his wife, a woman who had moved to the midlands from County Mayo as a young woman, who had died ten years before. Father Joseph finishes the rosary, waits silently for a while holding the man's hand, and gets up, conscious of having to return to church for the angelus bells, conscious the man might die the moment he walks through the door or go on for days yet. With a chorus of thank you, Fathers, the young priest leaves and weighs up the merits of the stairwell or the lift, they smell the same, thinks about how getting such decisions wrong were the difference sometimes between life and death growing up in Maputo, after the shooting started, weighs up how far 1990s Wolverhampton is from some kind of similar catastrophe, not so very far as everyone supposes, and goes for the lift.

In the bedroom, Billy stirs slightly, lifts his dry lips to his eldest daughter's ear as she leans over the bed to hear him speak,

"I was at North King Street," he says, "tell your mother when you see her that I'm sorry." They are his last words.

The Great Wolverhampton Novel smells of guilt and redemption. North King Street was a street in Dublin. At Easter 1916 it was on the edge of the area around the city's GPO held by the IRA during the Rising. Soldiers from the South Staffordshire Regiment, having lost fourteen men trying to advance down North King Street earlier in the week, rounded up fifteen men on a Friday afternoon and shot or bayoneted them, dumping their bodies in cellars. One more small massacre on an island of them. The soldiers killed, and those who did the killing, were from Wolverhampton and surrounding areas. Billy, who his family know as a hero of the Battle of the Menin Road Bridge at the end of the First World War, with his medals in a shoebox at the back of the kitchen cupboard, had returned to England in 1919, worked in various foundries, met a nice Irish girl named Edna at a tea dance, enjoyed his holiday in Rhyl every year, raised seven children, later eighteen grandchildren, at this point five great-grandchildren and a great-great-grandchild no one is yet aware of, lived his life as a quiet, family man, taking his wife to the church she helped clean three mornings a week, every Sunday, and sometimes to the early mass on a Wednesday.

Down on the street Father Joseph passes the young Billy Wright, says a quick prayer for forgiveness, as he steps out into the gutter and then across the road, as much to avoid the smell as the huddled figure himself, menacing though he also seems. Father Joseph casts a glance back, mistaking the homeless man for Fred, another homeless man, who lives in a tent on the ring road and for whom he often says prayers.

The Great Wolverhampton Novel often spirals and shifts into other stories, other lives, that of Fred, the ring-road tramp being one of them. There follows several chapters which follow the story of this figure of Wolverhampton history, real name Josef Stawinoga, with a meditation on the reasons for this man abandoning his life with a job at the steelworks in Bilston, his lost family in Poland, the curious rumours that used to surround him, not least that he had been a guard at Auschwitz (completely unfounded, but sometimes whispered with a kind of perverse glee in Black Country pubs of the era), though that he had lived through the horrors of the Second World War is undoubtedly true, his being adopted by local Hindus and Sikhs as a kind of Sidhu or holy man, and so on.

The Great Wolverhampton Novel is like a painting by Rita Donagh a map of the city street's always has the map of somewhere else showing through: Ireland, Poland, Pakistan and a hundred other places besides.

Meanwhile, by following his nose, the young Billy Wright is drawn closer and closer to the flat in which his estranged family is gathered and his grandad lies dying. It turns out that the young Billy is haunted by violence too, a street fight which brought his youth to an abrupt end, in which he stabbed a young man in the leg with a broken bottle, hitting an artery, during a street fight between white and Asian lads, and which he—wrongly—assumes to have caused the young man's death. He remembers the trail of blood as the kid hobbled up the street in front of him and into the back door of a shop which sold bright coloured material for saris. The smell of a terrible fear, both the boy's and his own. Billy had run too. When he returned to the shop a few days later the place was boarded up, gone, as if it had never been there at all. When he asked neighbours what had happened, what had happened to the family who lived there, "Trouble," he was told, "they've gone." So he went too, and never went home again, although never strayed too far either, careful not to be spotted, sleeping in old factories and drinking on the towpath of the cut.

The Great Wolverhampton Novel has several different versions, in some there follows a whole other epic, family story of a village just a few miles from the Line of Control high in the snow in Kashmir, and a family who end up in the back streets of Blakenhall, not doing so badly at all through the years, really, making a home in spite of Enoch Powell and all that, with a son who gets into the occasional fight but nothing too heavy, until a daughter gets pregnant with a local black boy and they move away to stay with family in Small Heath in Birmingham, pretty much as far as they will ever travel, and get things sorted out, which involves the birth of a beautiful baby girl, raised by her grandparents whom she thinks are her parents, with an aunty who always looks out for her, and another uncle with a vicious scar on his leg, who works as a barrister in London and often sends her books to read.

The Great Wolverhampton Novel then sometimes narrates various massacres associated with the town, not least the battle of Woden's Field in 910, which is one reason how it comes to smell of so much blood, whole rivers of them, so much iron, Saxon and Viking in this case, and an account of the riots following the death of Clinton McCurbin in police custody in Wolverhampton in 1987. There are other chapters which return to Blakenhall and narrate the scene at St. Luke's School on another 1990s morning when a man enters the playground with a machete and Lisa Potts covers the children in her care and no one dies. The Great Wolverhampton Novel confirms the place as one of miracles, as well as everything else. Some versions of the Great Wolverhampton Novel confront the smell of something rotten head-on and give an account of Enoch Powell's life, his role as a Wolverhampton MP, the speech, and the people who supported his views as well as those who resisted. Billy Wright, who still lies dying in his bed high above Blakenhall, had no time for the man, of course, instilled common decency into his children as much as he could, had seen enough hatred, been part of it well enough, for one lifetime, kept it locked away inside him as well as he could.

So to cut a long story—and the Great Wolverhampton Novel, as yet unwritten, is very much that—the fading smell of methyl methacrylate works like incense in leading the young Billy Wright to his grandad's home in the hour of his death, to be reconciled with his mother, the old man's daughter, who is still mulling over the words about North King Street and thinking about how she may seek to forget them entirely, and we leave them rising, like the smells from the city streets, as if figures in a painting by Chagall, halfway to the sky.

There sometimes follows a brief epilogue, with the family another generation on, the young Billy Wright restored, with a child of his own on his shoulders, watching the Blakenhall flats being blown-up, demolished, on another morning early this century. And this whole chapter smells of dust.

6

Dancing with Dad

Wendy Crickard

walking the hot July streets
past a workshop which no longer serves its purpose
engine oil soaked into the broken tarmac
the sweet blue smell cloying on the air
trailing Woodbines and Old Spice
and you
and me
running to meet you down Waste Bank
and sliding
sliding on the stones
and your hands
warm and safe
and small foot on large foot
your old brown mac flies around you
white tie top hat and tails

W. Crickard (✉)
West Midlands, UK

and you sing
and waltz me round faster and faster
spinning past the Top Bell and Old Ben's
spinning
spinning out into the world
and you
slowing
slowing
and your old brown mac
hangs in the shed
sleeves curved to embrace your partner
oil lingers in the dust

7

Smell and Memory in the Black Country: The Snidge Scrumpin' Experiments

Sebastian Groes and Tom Mercer

Childhood memory of sweets coming off rations in 1955 … Village shop. (Male, aged 65+, smell of Teddy Grays)

Burying a dead bird with my friends in a field by my house. (Female, aged 25–34, smell of canal water)

Feeling car sick in a Ford Anglia (it made me feel sick again) … somewhere on the way to Barmouth. (Female, aged 45–54, smell of burnt rubber)

Nan cooking dinner in her small kitchen, sun shining, and she has her apron on. Big table pulled out in back room for Sunday dinner with trifle to follow. (Female, aged 45–54, smell of faggots)

Falling over in holiday and having a badly grazed knee. Being taken to a St. John's Ambulance Station and having my knee dressed with medicated

S. Groes (✉) · T. Mercer
University of Wolverhampton, Wolverhampton, UK

lotion and a large sticking plaster. (Female, aged 65+, smell of carbolic soap)

Cough mixture, as a child … Only living with my Gran. The memory gives me a warm feeling. (Female, aged 55–64, smell of paint)

Introduction: Proust in the Black Country

The above quotes come from participants of the *Snidge Scrumpin'* events that took place as part of the Being Human Festival 2018. The events were hosted at the Black Country Living Museum and Wolverhampton Art Gallery, and examined the connection between olfaction, memory and the Black Country region. Members of the public were invited to take part in a psychological experiment to find out two things: first, we wanted to know the specific smells that belong to the Black Country; secondly, we wanted to understand in detail the (childhood) memories associated with those particular Black Country smells. The analysis, which is outlined below, gave us specific and original insights into the life and mind of the Black Country:

- It is difficult to identify a smell, but especially for smell of burnt rubber and faggots, which are both smells that have strong associations with the West Midlands.[1]
- The smell of paint and Teddy Grays (which is an herbal tablet with an 'unmistakeable flavour'[2] whose recipe is secret) elicited higher quality memories in those who grew up in the Black Country in comparison to those who grew up elsewhere.
- The smell of paint and Teddy Grays elicited higher quality memories in those who grew up in the Black Country in comparison to those who grew up elsewhere.

Below you will find a more detailed exposition of the experiment and its results. But in order to understand the results of the *Snidge Scrumpin'*, we need to historicise and contextualise the experiments in the history of what is known as the 'Proust Phenomenon'. Smells—compared to other senses such as vision and hearing—have a privileged access to unlocking childhood memories.[3] It started with a novel written by French novelist Marcel Proust, who was particularly interested in understanding the mechanics of his own being—and the role memory played within it. The project led to a decennia-long exploration of his life, in over one million words (1,267,069 words to be exact). A conventional novel of 250 pages is usually 75,000 words. À la recherche du temps perdu (translated as In Search of Lost Time, 1913–1927), contains a striking passage early on in the novel, when Proust's middle-aged narrator, Marcel, sips a tea-spoon of tilleul (lime-blossom tea) mixed with crumbs of a petite madeleine cake. The taste and smell trigger scenes from his childhood: it takes him back to the old houses of the village where he grew up, to the streets where he was sent on errands, the squares and gardens and, finally, to his aunt Léonie's bedroom where he'd drink madeleine soaked tilleul:

And as soon as I had recognized the taste of the piece of madeleine dipped in lime-blossom tea that my aunt used to give me [...] immediately the old grey house on the street, where her bedroom was, came like a stage-set to attach itself to the little wing opening on to the garden that had been built for my parents behind it [...] and with the house the town, from morning to night and in all weathers, the Square, where they sent me before lunch, the streets where I went to do errands, the paths we took if the weather was fine. And as in the game in which the Japanese amuse themselves by filling a porcelain bowl with water and steeping in it little pieces of paper until then indistinct, which, the moment they are immersed in it, stretch and shape themselves, colour and differentiate, become flowers, houses, human figures, firm and recognisable, so now all the flowers in our garden and M. Swann's park, the water-lilies on the Vivonne, and the good people of the village and their little dwellings and the church and all of Combray and its surroundings, all of this which is assuming form and substance, emerged, town and garden alike, from my cup of tea.[4]

Since the publication of the novel, psychologists and neuroscientists have tried to understand and replicate what has become known as the Proust Phenomenon.[5] We now know that odours are better cues in triggering autobiographical memories than other stimuli. This is because of the direct connections olfaction has with parts of the limbic system involved in generating emotion and memory. The neural basis for olfaction is unique.[6] Smell is the only sense that bypasses the thalamic relay and has primary access to regions of the brain typically found to be active during emotional processing (the amygdala), long term memory formation (the hippocampus) and higher-order cognitive reasoning and evaluation (orbitofrontal cortex). It is this unusual neural makeup that has led many to speculate on the unique role olfaction plays in memory, emotion and higher-order cognition.

What Does the Proust Phenomenon Mean?

For Barry C. Smith, the immediate and involuntary recall ('cued recall') through an odour-invoked memory evokes interesting philosophical and scientific questions: 'Do odour memories really take us back to how things were, or do they just produce a conviction in us that this is how things were? After all, we can't go back and check whether our memories accurately match the remembered scene. Perhaps odour memories simply convey an intensely vivid sense of the past *as if* it was being re-experienced, rather in the way déjà vu makes us feel we have lived through this experience before'.[7] This is an interesting philosophical remark because it suggests that Proust leads us to an epistemological conundrum in the sense that we simply cannot know what the exact status is of the experience that is retrieved. The brain is a black box and we cannot fully understand the electro-chemical processes that occur inside the skull.

Proust shows us that emotions and sensations come before memories. When he drinks his tea, it takes him a long time before the autobiographical, semantic memory (the story of a memory) emerges. In the novel, the memories of Combray, its streets and parks and, finally, his grandmother's house, take six pages to 'unfold': retrieving a memory triggered by smell is actually hard work, because smells are hard to name and describe. Olfaction is known as the silent sense.[8] Although odours can trigger strong, emotional sensations that could become equally emotive memories, we have a hard time identifying smells—unless you belong to the Jahai, a community of hunter-gatherers living in the Malay Peninsula, who can name smells just as easy as colours.[9] Smell not only gives more emotional memories, but also different ones from verbal or visual information.[10] Scents are particularly good at evoking nostalgia—which will come as no surprise to readers of Proust, though the intricacies of the effect of olfaction on generating nostalgia are very detailed. And this nostalgia has many beneficial effects on people: 'Scent-evoked nostalgia predicted higher levels of positive affect, self-esteem, self-continuity, optimism, social connectedness and meaning in life'.[11]

For writers, smell is a challenge too, but history shows also that the literary mind is not only obsessed but also not badly equipped to capture smell in words. Perhaps most famously, Patrick Süskind's *Das Parfum* (1985) is a novel about the super-smeller Jean-Baptiste Grenouille who becomes a perfumer in eighteenth-century Paris; his obsession with olfaction leads him to undertake some extraordinary criminal acts. But throughout literary history writers are profoundly interested to capture smell, from the 'Sweet breathing Zephyrus' in Edmund Spenser's *Prothalamion* (1596) to T. S. Eliot's obsession with London's stench of death and excrement in *The Waste Land* (1922). Virginia Woolf's *Mrs Dalloway* (1925) comes to mind as well, where (the thought of) the smell of flowers sets in motion the Proustian, sensory and sensual memory maze contained in the stream of consciousness of the novel's protagonist, Clarissa Dalloway.

Proust's mentioning of a 'stage-set' highlights that memories are not real but fictional, imaginary experiences; there is something theatrical about memories. This is further developed by the reference to the 'little pieces of paper', which make the writing of memories an explicitly textual activity. Both metaphors foreground the fact that memories are representations of past experiences—not the real thing. A further important issue to notice here is Proust's emphasis on the spatiality of memories:

they may start off, perhaps, as a vague emotion, but they become more concrete when they are attached to 'real' physical spaces, objects and places. What is also interesting to note—and this is supported by the Snidge data—is that we can see a certain rippling effect: starting with a memory contained to an intimate, safe family space (his aunt's bedroom), the memory starts to spread outwards, coming to absorb more and more places, public buildings, paths—until the entire town is evoked. This rippling effect also takes place in temporal terms: Proust mentions a scene 'in all weathers', suggesting that a temporal palimpsest is generated. In short, memories and the retrieving of memories, is a highly artificial business.

The Proust Phenomenon shows that literature is capable of allowing different disciplines to speak to one another. Neuroscience can explain why smell is a strong trigger, and psychology can show which stimuli have particularly vivid and emotional effects, but literature has an equally important role to play in revealing how memory works. We might argue that without literature, emotions remain silenced, that literature is the key to giving voice to the silent sense.

The Proust Phenomenon's wider significance is not only to do with nostalgia for our personal, subjective past: by triggering strong, emotive childhood memories, we are being reconnected with our former selves, with the selves that we (may) have forgotten. This process is beneficial because it gives us a different perspective upon our lives—which afford us the possibility of perspective and contemplation. These moments confront us with our younger selves, perhaps different, more innocent, and thus asks questions about selfhood and causation—we come to wonder how we ended up where we are now—what life choices, motives and desires have brought us where we find ourselves today.

Indeed, in a nicely multidisciplinary essay written by a literary scholar and a neuroscientist, Kirsten Shepherd-Barr and Gordon M. Shepherd note something important about the madeleine episode in connection with not only the meaning of life but also about our understanding of the self:

Proust himself firming believes in an inner truth that can be extracted from beneath the encrustations of self-delusion, if only we may experience moments like that of the madeleine, which puts us back in touch with our true selves. He clings on to an ultimately Romantic belief in an inner reality and truth that are unchanging and hidden, if only we can find the key to unlock them; this contrasts with the idea of a constantly changing version of ourselves from which we get farther and farther way by our ever more elaborate "mental maps."[12]

Although one may question whether Proust's attitude is that of a Romantic, but it certainly is Platonic, and his work should be seen as a deep, complex quest for understanding the self by unpeeling layer and layer of superficial memory matter until we arrive at what today is mostly deemed an old-fashioned idea—the soul—which in modernity has gradually become replaced with memory, as Ian Hacking argues.[13]

Our sense of smell is a key component in our behaviour and mental lives. Recent science has shown that there is a strong relationship between olfaction and depression, for instance: 'patients with depression have reduced olfactory performance when compared with the healthy controls and conversely, patients with olfactory dysfunction, have symptoms of depression that worsen with severity of smell loss'.[14] Smell is also related to our stress levels. Women feel calmer after being exposed to their male partner's scent. Conversely, a stranger's smell has the opposite effect, raising levels of cortisol, the stress hormone.[15] Pheromones are important in women's sexuality: pheromones may be present in all bodily secretions but most attention has been geared towards axillary sweat which contains the odorous 16-androstenes. One of these steroidal compounds, androstadienone, is present at much higher concentrations in male sweat and can be detected by women, albeit with wide variation in sensitivity. Upper-lip application of a pharmacological dose of androstadienone results in improved mood and heightened focus— particularly to capture emotional information. A positive mood is known to facilitate women's sexual response, and increased focus improves sexual satisfaction. Indeed, some studies showed a beneficial effect of androstadienone on sexual desire and arousal. In conclusion, some data indicate that 16-androstene pheromones, in particular androstadienone, play a beneficial role in women's mood, focus and sexual response and perhaps also in mate selection. There is also a practice such as scent marketing:

scents can persuade customers to stay in retail spaces longer and browse more, improve their sense of quality and create a warm feeling of familiarity. Nike scents stores to increase intent to purchase by 80%; some petrol stations' mini-marts pump coffee smell into the air to see coffee purchases rise by 300%.

Smell awareness is therefore crucial to our individual being and to our cultures. In a cautionary tale, 'The Name, The Nose' (1986), Italo Calvino warns against the loss of our olfactory consciousness: 'the noseless man of the future' will lose emotions and have a reduced ability to make sense of life altogether. In modernity we are living in a culture subjected to a changing, often growing regime of hygiene, driven by a politico-capitalist elite and a powerful middle-class culture that propagated their sociocultural values, amongst others, by means of a specific politics of smell. Marginalised parts of the population, including the working classes, women and ethnic minorities have been subject to olfactory discrimination. The working classes were automatically associated with stench, as the level of cleanliness was metaphorically associated with social status. Historically, women have been told to artificially scent their bodies and, since 1915, shave their body hair with a view to reduce body odour. Ethnic minorities have an equally ambitious position in the olfactory imaginary: the Orientalising western, white, priviledged perception exoticised the Other and associated the non-western body with uncleanliness. The white, male-dominated heteronormative tradition of Humanism and the legacy of the Enlightenment—underpinned by the privileged position that made male sensory perception central and women's bodies and perception invisible or at least marginal—have focused their dominance also via sensory ideological powerplay. During late capitalism and the start of the twenty-first century, these olfactory politics of ideological oppression, exploitation and manipulation continue to grow. We must cultivate a smell awareness to become more conscious of olfactory practices within modern culture. This is the subject of another book, but suffice it to say that it is not wholly a coincidence that the Snidge Scrumpin' experiment are taking place in a part of the world that is overlooked and neglected.

Snidge Scrumpin's Method

To investigate the connection between smell, memory and place, an interactive experiment was designed and informed by prior work into autobiographical odour memory. However, unlike past psychological research into the Proust Phenomenon, this experiment aimed to assess the effects of specific smells on memory recall in relation to a specific region: the Black Country. This design therefore moves away from past work that has focussed on comparing smells against other memory cues (e.g. words or pictures), and towards an assessment of smell itself. The experiment compared smells belonging to the Black Country region against more generic smells, to see which odours prompted recall. It also examined the participants themselves, particularly concerning where they grew up and how this related to autobiographical odour memory. Fifty-two participants volunteered for the experiment (35 at the Black Country Living Museum and 17 at Wolverhampton Art Gallery), including 23 men and 29 women. All of the participants provided written informed consent after the procedure was explained and questions answered.

The majority of participants identified as White British (81% of the sample) and most were aged 45 or over. More demographic information is shown in Tables 7.1 and 7.2. Participants also reported their place of birth and residence during childhood and adolescence, along with their current residence (see Table 7.3).

It was important to determine whether participants were local to the Black Country, which was classed as the regions in and surrounding

Table 7.1 Number of participants according to ethnicity

Ethnicity	Frequency
White British	42
Black or Black British Caribbean	1
Mixed White/Black Caribbean	1
White Irish	1
Black or Black British African	1
Other Asian background	1
Other White background	5

Table 7.2 Number of participants according to age

Age category	Frequency
18–24	2
25–34	3
35–44	7
45–54	14
55–64	10
65+	16

Table 7.3 Frequency of location according to age

Location	Birth place	Childhood	Adolescence	Present
UK				
Black Country	26	24	23	35
East Midlands	0	0	0	1
East of England	0	1	2	0
London	4	0	0	0
North East	1	1	1	0
North West	2	1	1	0
Other UK	1	1	0	0
Other West Midlands	5	9	12	11
South East	4	2	2	2
South West	0	1	2	2
Yorkshire and the Humber	2	2	1	0
Varied UK	N/A	3	1	1
Abroad				
Europe	4	3	3	0
Outside Europe	3	3	3	0
Varied UK/International	N/A	1	1	0

Wolverhampton, Walsall, Dudley and West Bromwich, or elsewhere. As there is a geographical overlap between the Black Country and the West Midlands, the West Midlands was categorised as regions in and around Birmingham, along with Herefordshire, Shropshire, Staffordshire, Warwickshire and Worcestershire, but not any of the Black Country regions.

From the responses provided, 24 individuals were classed as having grown up in the Black Country (having spent their childhood there) and 28 had grown up elsewhere. This was particularly important, given the possible connections between smell and childhood memory, and this grouping was used in the analysis of the data. Table 7.3 provides a full breakdown of location responses.

The task required participants to experience and evaluate a series of smells, and then attempt to recall a memory evoked by each smell. Eight different smells were created for the task, including four general smells (lemon, paint, curry paste and carbolic soap) and four Black Country smells (canal water, burnt rubber, Teddy Grays herbal tablets and faggots). The smells were located in small, numbered tubs, but the content was obscured.

Participants had to select one of the tubs, open it and smell the contents. There was no visual information to help them and the contents were not revealed in advance—that way, participants only experienced the smell, without other cues. After smelling the tub's contents, participants tried to identify and name the smell, and were encouraged to guess if they were unsure. They recorded their answer in a booklet. Next, they rated the smell on its familiarity, intensity and pleasantness using a seven-point scale (where 1 indicated 'Not at all' and 7 indicated 'Very').

Once the smell had been rated, participants were asked to describe any memory evoked by the smell. If they were able to do this, they provided a short description of the event and attempted to state their age at the time. Next, they rated the memory on its significance, detail and pleasantness, again using a seven-point scale. The final question assessed whether the memory could be tied to a specific place or location, and whether the memory came from blind smelling the tub or after the name was revealed (in the vast majority of cases, responses were to the blind smelling).

This procedure was then repeated until all of the smells had been experienced. Participants completed the task in small groups and typically needed 45 min to finish the task. At this point, the contents of each tub were revealed, and participants were asked to make a note of any other smells and memories they associated with the Black Country.

The Results

Five major areas were explored when analysing the data:

- The ability to identify smells;
- How the smells were rated;
- The ability of smells to evoke autobiographical memories;
- The age at which recalled memories were formed;
- How recalled memories were rated.

Descriptive and inferential statistics were used to explore the data, with statistically significant findings ($p < 0.05$) being outlined below. There were seven major highlights:

1. It is difficult to identify a smell, but especially for smells of burnt rubber and faggots;
2. Familiar smells are likely to be rated as intense and pleasant, and are better at eliciting memories;
3. The smell of paint and Teddy Grays herbal tablets were particularly successful at prompting memories;
4. Memories recalled in response to the smells were overwhelmingly likely to come from childhood;
5. The smell of paint and Teddy Grays elicited higher quality memories in those who grew up in the Black Country in comparison to those who grew up elsewhere;
6. Women rated smells as more intense than men, on average;
7. Those aged between 45 and 54 recalled a greater number of memories than those aged 65 and over.

Identifying Smells

Participants' ability to correctly identify the content of each tub was assessed. Scoring of responses was lenient, with roughly accurate answers being classed as correct. However, an absent response was classed as incorrect. From this, the proportion of smells correctly identified was calculated, but participants were correct less than half of the time (44%,

Table 7.4 Mean proportion of responses (and standard deviation) for correctly identifying each smell

Smell	Mean proportion correct
Lemon	0.56 (0.50)
Canal water	0.52 (0.50)
Paint*	0.67 (0.47)
Burnt rubber*	0.11 (0.32)
Teddy Grays herbal tablets	0.56 (0.50)
Curry paste	0.44 (0.50)
Carbolic soap	0.50 (0.50)
Faggots*	0.17 (0.38)

Note A Chi-square test was used to compare the number of participants who did and did not recall a memory in response to each smell. * = significant result

on average). Yet there were differences depending on the type of smell being used—participants were less likely to correctly identify Black Country smells than general smells (35 vs. 54%, respectively).

A more detailed analysis was then used to examine responses to each individual smell. As shown in Table 7.4, the smells of burnt rubber and faggots were particularly hard to identify, though over two-thirds of the participants correctly identified the smell of paint.

Rating the Smells

Each smell was rated on its familiarity, intensity and pleasantness, and descriptive statistics are shown in Table 7.5. Smells could be rated on a scale of 1–7. Matching the analysis above, the smell of burnt rubber was rated as less familiar than all other smells, and less intense than the smell of paint and Teddy Grays. The smell of faggots was also rated as less intense than paint and Teddy Grays. Further differences were revealed when considering the pleasantness of the smells—lemon and Teddy Grays were rated as more pleasant than most other smells, whereas the smells of canal water and burnt rubber were rated as less pleasant than most other smells. Interestingly, positive correlations were found amongst the three factors. So, a smell rated as highly familiar was also likely to be rated as high in intensity and pleasantness.

Table 7.5 Mean ratings (standard deviation) of familiarity, intensity and pleasantness for each smell

Smell	Familiarity	Intensity	Pleasantness
Lemon	5.25 (1.67)	5.23 (1.29)	5.44 (1.40)
Canal water	4.90 (1.57)	5.08 (1.51)	3.08 (1.51)
Paint	5.78 (1.31)	5.74 (1.26)	3.71 (1.80)
Burnt rubber	3.77 (1.95)	4.61 (1.71)	2.79 (1.40)
Teddy Grays herbal tablets	5.68 (1.54)	5.76 (1.20)	5.47 (1.43)
Curry paste	4.90 (1.77)	5.42 (1.64)	4.21 (1.83)
Carbolic soap	4.76 (1.99)	5.32 (1.57)	4.02 (1.86)
Faggots	5.33 (1.51)	4.98 (1.42)	4.78 (1.58)

Note One-way repeated measures ANOVAs were used to compare the eight smells on their ratings of familiarity, intensity and pleasantness. Significant main effects were explored using Sidak post hoc tests

When grouping the smells as either Black Country or general, and factoring in the place the participant had spent their childhood, further effects emerged. Black Country smells were rated as less familiar, less intense and less pleasant than general smells. However, those who grew up in the Black Country did rate the smells as more familiar overall, and women rated the smells as more intense than men, on average.

Remembering the Past

For each smell, participants' ability to recall a memory was determined. On average, participants were able to recall a memory to 60% of the smells, but there was a lot of variability. Some participants did not recall any memories, whereas others recalled memories in response to every smell. If participants were able to correctly identify a smell, they were more likely to recall a memory, and this was especially likely for familiar smells.

Further analyses were used to examine the ability of Black Country and general smells to elicit memories. Whilst no effects were found for this global analysis, examination of specific smells did reveal some interesting outcomes.

Paint and Teddy Grays were particularly effective at evoking memories, as shown in Fig. 7.1. Almost three-quarters of participants recalled

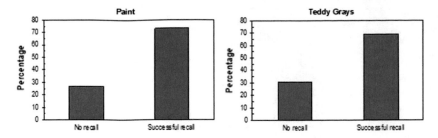

Fig. 7.1 Percentage of participants recalling or failing to recall a memory in response to the smell of paint and Teddy Grays. These two smells were most effective at eliciting memories

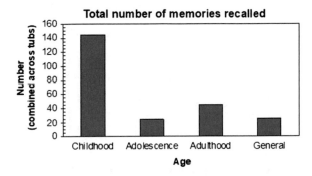

Fig. 7.2 Total number of memories recalled across all smells and participants, according to the age at which the memory was formed

a memory in response to the smell of paint, and around 70% did so for the smell of Teddy Grays.

Furthermore, the memories recalled were overwhelmingly likely to come from childhood. Based on the answers given, it was possible to determine how old the participant was when the remembered event occurred. Four groups were used, including childhood (up to the age of 12), adolescence (13–19 years old), adulthood (20 years old or over) and general (where no specific memory was recalled, but a general theme may have been remembered). As highlighted in Fig. 7.2, when a memory was recalled, it usually dated to childhood. More specific analyses showed that this effect applied to every smell, with the exception of paint, which yielded a similar number of childhood and adulthood memories.

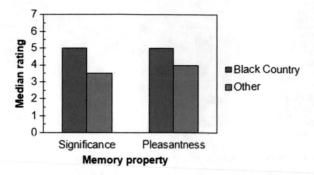

Fig. 7.3 Ratings of the significance and pleasantness of memories recalled in response to the smell of paint according to whether participants spent their childhood in the Black Country (blue columns) or another location (orange columns)

Finally, the quality of the memories was examined by looking at how they were rated (as participants were not able to recall a memory to every smell, there was less data available and non-parametric statistics were used). When an event was remembered, participants rated the significance, detail and pleasantness of the memory. Particularly interesting outcomes were found for the smells of paint and Teddy Grays. Those who grew up in the Black Country rated the significance and pleasantness of the memory evoked by paint as higher than those who grew up elsewhere (see Fig. 7.3). Similarly, the significance and detail of the memories evoked by the smell of Teddy Grays was higher for those who grew up in the Black Country than those who grew up elsewhere. This is depicted in Fig. 7.4.

Age Differences

Participants were arranged into four groups based on their age: 18–44 ($N = 12$), 45–54 ($N = 15$), 55–64 ($N = 10$) or 65 and over ($N = 16$). Age differences were found in response to the ratings of the smells, with smells being rated as less intense and pleasant in those aged 18–44 than those aged 45–54. Those aged 45–54 also rated the smells as more pleasant than all other age groups.

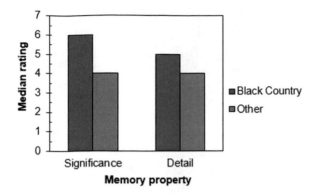

Fig. 7.4 Ratings of the significance and detail of memories recalled in response to the smell of Teddy Grays according to whether participants spent their childhood in the Black Country (blue columns) or another location (orange columns)

Age differences were also found in the ability to recall an event in response to the past. This was primarily because those aged 65 or over remembered fewer events than those aged 45–54.

Describing the Past

The numerical data outlined above provides useful information about the connections between smell, memory and place. But examination of the written responses can yield deeper insights. When considering childhood memories, it was clear that they could be highly vivid and detailed, even though the original event may have happened decades ago. A common theme was family—which is a connection anticipated by Marcel Proust's description of the madeleine effect, which brings him back to his grandmother. Consider the following responses to smells from participants in the experiment:

> I lived with my Gran for many years as a child and she would dish up faggots quite often as they were cheap. (Female, aged 55–64, smell of faggots)

Going to do-it-all DIY outlet on a Saturday morning with my father. The day was over-cast. (Male, aged 35–44, smell of paint)

...it reminds me of having pancakes with lemon and sugar. Homemade by Mom of course ... Our family kitchen, which was quite the most frequently used room in the home. (Female, aged 45–54, smell of lemon)

Cleaning out a shed with my Dad ... at home in the village we lived in. (Male, aged 65+, smell of canal water)

Making lemon marmalade with my mum, cutting up the fruit and cooking it. (Female, aged 65+, smell of lemon)

Having fruit after dinner as a child ... with my siblings – large family we used to half our oranges to share. (Female, aged 45–54, smell of lemon).

Having a cold as a child, my Mum rubbed this on my chest, tucked me up in bed with a hot water bottle. (Female, aged 45–54, smell of lemon)

We had a paraffin heather in the hall of the house where I lived as a child. It was a strong smell in our house and caused lots of condensation. (Female, aged 45–54, smell of burnt rubber)

One participant recalled the following memory in response to the smell of lemon: '...it reminds me of having pancakes with lemon and sugar. Homemade by mom of course'. Indeed, as well as eliciting memories of family members (usually parents or grandparents), the place could be vividly evoked too. For example, one participant clearly remembered her grandmother's kitchen in response to the smell of faggots: 'Nan cooking dinner in her small kitchen, sun shining, and she has her apron on. Big table pulled out in back room for Sunday dinner with trifle to follow'. Others remembered specific features of the family home. For instance, one participant remembered the house's hall in response to the smell of burnt rubber: 'We had a paraffin heather in the hall of the house where I lived as a child. It was a strong smell in our house and caused lots of condensation'. Memory of other locations were common too. Examples included a garden ('The smell reminds me of my childhood garden, the bottom of which had a lot of strawberry beds, soil, etc.'), a shed ('Cleaning out a shed with my Dad ... at home in the village we lived in') and a town ('Walking to school and going to the sweet shop ... the row of shops'). The memories were usually rated as pleasant too, and this could be observed in the written summaries, e.g. '...living with my Gran. The memory gives me a warm feeling'.

Proust would have recognised himself in this description.

Notes

1. Burnt rubber is associated with the smell emanating from the Goodyear Tyre factory in Wolverhampton between 1929 and the 1970s. Faggots are meatballs produced from minced off-cuts and offal (especially pork) mixed together with herbs and breadcrumbs. It is a traditional dish in Wales and the English Midlands.

2. Teddy Grays's website claims: 'Edward Grays of Dudley herbal tablets are made using a secret family recipe, which has being passed down from generation to generation. Many companies have attempted to make our herbal tablets but none have managed to recreate our unmistakable flavour - no herbal tablet tastes like ours!' http://www.teddygrays.co.uk [Accessed 29 July 2019].

3. See Simon Chu and John J. Downes, 'Odour-Evoked Autobiographical Memories: Psychological Investigations of Proustian Phenomena', *Chemical Senses* 25, no. 1 (2000): 111–116. See also, Maaike J. de Bruijn and Michael Bender, 'Olfactory Cues Are More Effective Than Visual Cues in Experimentally Triggering Autobiographical Memories', *Memory* 26, no. 4 (2017): 547–558.

4. Marcel Proust, *In Search of Lost Time—Volume 1* (London: Penguin, 2003), 50.

5. See, for instance, Johan Willander and Maria Larsson, 'Olfaction and Emotion: The Case of Autobiographical Memory', *Memory & Cognition* 35, no. 7 (October 2007): 1659–1663.

6. See, for example, Y. Soudry et al., 'Olfactory System and Emotion: Common Substrates', *European Annals of Otorhinolaryngology, Head and Neck Diseases* 128, no. 1 (January 2011): 18–23. https://doi.org/10.1016/j.anorl.2010.09.007.

7. Barry C. Smith, 'Proust, the Madeleine and Memory', in *Memory in the Twenty-First Century*, edited by S. Groes (London: Palgrave Macmillan, 2016), 38.
8. See Draaisma 2004.
9. See the research of Asifa Majid. For instance, https://www.ru.nl/english/news-agenda/news/vm/language-studies/2018/hunter-gatherers-special-way-smells/.
10. See Maria Larsson and Johan Willander, 'Autobiographical Odor Memory', International Symposium on Olfaction and Taste. *Annals of the New York Academy of Sciences* 1170 (2009): 318–232.
11. See R. A. Reid et al., 'Scent-Evoked Nostalgia', *Memory* 23, no. 2 (2015): 157–166, 155. https://doi.org/10.1080/09658211.2013.876048.
12. Kirsten Shepherd-Barr and Gordon M. Shepherd, 'Madeleines and Neuro-modernism: Reassessing Mechanisms of Autobiographical Memory in Proust', *a/b: Auto/Biography Studies* 13, no. 1 (Spring 1998): 47.
13. See Ian Hacking, *Rewriting the Soul: Multiple Personality and the Sciences of Memory* (Princeton: Princeton University Press, 1995), 5.
14. See P. Kohli et al., 'The Association Between Olfaction and Depression: A Systematic Review', *Chemical Senses* 41, no. 6 (July 2016): 479–486. https://doi. org/10.1093/chemse/bjw061.
15. See M. Hofer et al., 'Olfactory Cues from Romantic Partners and Strangers Moderate Women's Responses to Stress', *Journal of Personality and Social Psychology* 114, no. 1 (January 2018): 1–9.

Works Cited

Chu, Simon and John J. Downes. 'Odour-Evoked Autobiographical Memories: Psychological Investigations of Proustian Phenomena', *Chemical Senses* 25, no. 1 (2000).
de Bruijn, Maaike J. and Michael Bender. 'Olfactory Cues Are More Effective Than Visual Cues in Experimentally Triggering Autobiographical Memories', *Memory* 26, no. 4 (2017): 547–558.
Hacking, Ian. *Rewriting the Soul: Multiple Personality and the Sciences of Memory* (Princeton: Princeton University Press, 1995).

Hofer, M. et al., 'Olfactory Cues from Romantic Partners and Strangers Moderate Women's Responses to Stress', *Journal of Personality and Social Psychology,* 114, no. 1 (January 2018): 1–9.

Kohli, P. et al., 'The Association Between Olfaction and Depression: A Systematic Review', *Chemical Senses* 41, no. 6 (July 2016): 479–486. https://doi.org/10.1093/chemse/bjw061.

Larsson, Maria and Johan Willander. 'Autobiographical Odor Memory', International Symposium on Olfaction and Taste. *Annals of the New York Academy of Sciences* 1170 (2009).

Proust, Marcel. *In Search of Lost Time—Volume 1* (London: Penguin, 2003).

Reid, R. A. et al., 'Scent-Evoked Nostalgia', *Memory* 23, no. 2. (2015): 157–166, 155. https://doi.org/10.1080/09658211.2013.876048.

Shepherd-Barr, Kirsten and Gordon M. Shepherd. 'Madeleines and Neuromodernism: Reassessing Mechanisms of Autobiographical Memory in Proust', *a/b: Auto/Biography Studies* 13, no. 1 (Spring 1998).

Smith, Barry. C. 'Proust, the Madeleine and Memory', in *Memory in the Twenty-First Century,* edited by S. Groes (London: Palgrave Macmillan, 2016).

Soudry, Y. et al. 'Olfactory System and Emotion: Common Substrates', *European Annals of Otorhinolaryngology, Head and Neck Diseases* 128, no. 1 (January 2011): 18–23. https://doi.org/10.1016/j.anorl.2010.09.007.

Willander, Johan and Maria Larsson. 'Olfaction and Emotion: The Case of Autobiographical Memory', *Memory & Cognition* 35, no. 7 (October 2007).

8

What Does a Black Country Childhood Smell of?

Kerry Hadley-Pryce

There is an elegant, industrial quality to any Black Country childhood memory. Of course. But think of the smell of dogs and damp carpets and mix in a sense of baking bread and cooling pastries, and ripe apples and warm shoe leather and disinfectant, and think of that smell as something bright orange and glossy and clean, and you're in Brierley Hill Market, or I am. Think of a burnt cream smell, toffee-thick and lingering, and you're experiencing the exotic smell of sugar-beet, wafting in all the way from Stourport through Kidderminster and through your windows into where you live. On other days, on other winds, that horseblankety, musty, wet-metalness arrives like something creeping, from Tipton or Dudley. It lies a little heavy inside you, it sticks inside your nose, inside your head with the frequency of a singing bowl. And then, on Saturday afternoons, the scalded milkish smell of the icecream van. Mrs. Harris—she made her own and her son drove round our estate in a hired van that chugged out diesel in grey, like a magic trail. And there are breweries—a few—The

K. Hadley-Pryce (✉)
University of Wolverhampton, Wolverhampton, UK

S. Groes et al. (eds.), *Smell, Memory, and Literature in the Black Country*,
https://doi.org/10.1007/978-3-030-57212-9_8

Bull & Bladder, Ma Pardoe's, Banks's. Layers of piney, grassy bananary air. It's your Dad's breath on a Sunday afternoon, that is, like velvet being flapped, warming the place, then lying heavy. This smell, you think you're never going to stop experiencing it. It's more than just your history, it's like it becomes part of your biology. It's like it becomes a bulky weight you carry around with you, taking a place in your memory. In the summer, the factories clang with men's voices, slick with oil and fire, breathing out something primitive and vaguely thrilling. And of a Friday lunchtime, when factory workers finish early, take a breath outside a pub, the smell of beer like smouldering leaves is mesmerising. And everybody is smoking cigarettes, of course, and all that excites the moment you're in. Your granny's house smells of coal-dust and woodbines and imperial leather and camomile tea to settle her nerves, and there or thereabouts there is a mashed-potato smell from next door, because it's Monday's bubble & squeak. She sends you to the Outdoor, your granny does, to get your grandad's after-work beer: two pints of Banks's mild poured into a pop bottle, and even though the place is clean, the smell of dust and sweat is sour and earthy and bread-like, and because you're young, you imagine that's what men will smell like, close to. And Christmases had their own smells: your dad pours whisky into a Stuart-Crystal cut-glass tumbler—only the one—and though it looks like something precious, this liquid gold, this Christmas drink, and he holds it like you've seen people on films hold similar glasses, to you, it smells of wet cardboard in bin lorries, or Brasso and orange peel, but it—that smell—it will always remind you of your dad at Christmas.

When Indian takeaways take up empty shops, it's suddenly exotic, like you're not in the Black Country any more. Close your eyes and breathe in all those spices. It's almost medicinal, sharp. It billows out and around you, like it's goading you to travel, to leave, but you still like the ripe tang of cooking oil being heated, and potatoes being chopped and fish being battered and peas being mushed, and though you can't find the words sometimes, it doesn't matter, not really. Just take a breath, breathe in the smells and breathe out your memories.

9

The Smell of Black Country 'chai'

Narinder Dhami

My dad arrived in the UK in 1954, and was followed by quite a few members of his extended family. Many of them settled around Wolverhampton, and also a little further afield in Birmingham and Coventry. Sunday was visiting-day, the day when my mum and dad would pack their three kids into the car and head for one relatives' house after another to chat, catch up and drink tea.

Tea… How my ten-year-old heart would sink down into my sensible flat sandals when tea was offered and accepted (it was impossible to refuse—it would have been as shocking as expressing support for the National Front). I would hear the clatter of saucepans in the kitchen and feel even more depressed, knowing that I'd have to take at least a few sips or be considered really rude (another no-no).

The smell of that tea is something I've never forgotten. The tea leaves and milk were boiled on the stove, along with fragrant spices. Although we ate curry at home, back then I couldn't identify the slightly nutty,

N. Dhami (✉)
Shropshire, UK

© The Author(s), under exclusive license to Springer
Nature Switzerland AG 2021
S. Groes et al. (eds.), *Smell, Memory, and Literature in the Black Country*,
https://doi.org/10.1007/978-3-030-57212-9_9

sweet spice with the aromatic smell that was mostly used to make the 'chai'. I know now that it was cardamom, and whenever I smell that now, I'm taken right back to the 1970s. Sometimes a tin of condensed milk was used to make the tea, and the scent was then even more mind-blowingly sweet, almost tangible. It was too much even for a ten-year-old's palate, and we'd end up sneakily passing our cups to our (English) mum, who would valiantly drink the lot.

Indian 'chai' is now a regular on the menus of coffee-shops like Starbucks. But my Indian relatives mostly no longer drink it and use ordinary old teabags. Perversely, I miss being offered it when I go to visit. But I haven't yet plucked up the courage to order it in Starbucks.

10

'Pack up Your Blarting': The Language of the Senses in Black Country Dialect

Esther Asprey

Senses and Dialect—An Introduction

The novelist Anthony Cartwright draws on the deprivation and pollution surrounding Dudley in his 2009 novel *Heartland* set in that town (fictionalised as Cinderheath) in his imaginings of sight in the area:

> A bloke from Tipton goes to New York for his holiday, decides to visit Ground Zero, yer know, pay his respects. He's stondin lookin at the ruins an this chap comes up to him, big ten-gallon hat, typical Yank, from Texas, like Bush, yer know.
> Hey Pardner, this bloke says.
> How do, says the bloke from Tipton.
> Where the hell you all from?
> Me? I'm from Tipton, mate.
> Tipton? Tipton? What the hell state's that in?

E. Asprey (✉)
University of Warwick, Coventry, UK

© The Author(s), under exclusive license to Springer
Nature Switzerland AG 2021
S. Groes et al. (eds.), *Smell, Memory, and Literature in the Black Country*,
https://doi.org/10.1007/978-3-030-57212-9_10

Our bloke has a look around him an says, Abaht the same bloody state as this.[1] (p. 1)

The Black Country, though it does not exist in one official county (or state, as the American would have it), is said by Cartwright to be 'in a state.' It has suffered the ravages of industrial decline post WW2 and many boroughs now rank among the highest in the UK for social deprivation.[2] Concomitantly, the local dialect associated with the region has been the butt of many jokes, and ranks low on psychosocial models correlating dialect with prestige and intelligence.[3] Even the name of the region and its identity were forged (literally and metaphorically) during the Industrial Revolution, and the region is named for the severe air pollution it suffered. It is therefore an interesting region and language variety to examine, since on the surface it would seem that negative sensory experiences might proliferate there.

Between 2002 and 2006 I carried out fieldwork in the Black Country, interviewing 68 people in the region and recording their dyadic conversations with each other as they discussed the words they used in their everyday life, and words they associated with the region. The conversation revealed that Black Country dialect is in widespread use, despite the stigma a process of standardisation in English has resulted in for dialects across Britain and Ireland. It also revealed that although processes operate on dialect which result in some words and grammatical structures falling from use, in fact the dialect is vital and speakers continue to coin new words to describe their experiences in the world, they borrow new words from other speech communities, and they update words and sayings so that those words and sayings better reflect the changing experiences of life in the region. In this chapter, I examine possible models of how the sensory organs are connected, and look at how dialect speakers and dialect writers use lexis and sayings to encode their own sensory experiences in the Black Country across time, before coming to some conclusions about the future of Black Country dialect and the changing sensory experiences which unfold across the region. I start by examining models of sensory experience since antiquity.

Models of Sensory Experience

Bodo Winter[4] reports that traditionally western linguistics divides up the senses into five; these correspond to the so-called Aristotelian senses: touch, taste, hearing, sight and smell. He problematises this:

> The five-fold way of carving up the sensory space furthermore does not correspond directly to everything we know from neurophysiology and perceptual psychology. Scientists recognize many subdivisions that do not fall neatly into the categories of sight, sound, touch, taste, and smell [...] For example, researchers recognize that pain is separate from other dimensions of touch: Pain perception is supported by underlying brain structures that are separate from regular touch perception [...] Indeed, most researchers think of pain ("nociception") as a separate sense. Similarly, the so-called "vomeronasal organ" may be involved in constituting another sense that is different from the Aristotelian senses. This organ, partially separated from regular olfaction, is responsible for the perception of pheromones [...] These are but two of many examples which fall through the cracks.

He continues:

> Not only are there many different criteria from which to choose, but each criterion itself is fuzzy. For example, what do we consider as a "body organ"? How are we to deal with distributed organs, such as the skin, or sensory systems that span the entire body, such as the internal senses? Do we treat neural tissue as being part of a sense? If so, the distinctions between the senses become even more messy, because the brain is massively interconnected. If we follow the receptor-based criterion, what divisions do we make? Should we treat mechanical perception and temperature perception as two separate senses because they are associated with their own receptors? But then, what about the many different types of mechanical receptors, with some receptors specializing in slow or fast vibrations, others in the perception of sustained touch, and still others in the perception of skin stretching? Shall we assign separate senses to each one of these receptors? These questions show the difficulty of establishing criteria for what constitutes a sense.

Notwithstanding the issues with this system, since we are looking at a dialect that is a variety of a language in the global West, it is not unreasonable to start from the assumption that the five senses system is a well embedded starting point for Black Country speakers and writers examining linguistic encoding of sensory experience., though it would be wise to remember that others are now broadening out sensory models to include up to 23 senses, and to expect the sensory experiences they map to be hard to place in a five senses mode.

This chapter now examines memories of the Black Country as it was and as it is now, by examining sensory encodings, and it does this by prioritising oral and written testimonies about the area and its associated dialect. The Black Country is by no means without a literary tradition, though like all other areas across the British Isles, its regional language variety is viewed on a national level (in exams, in high earning workplaces, in the court system) as deficient when compared to written and spoken Standard English. There is a rich vein of written and spoken sources charting the dialect of the area which contains words we might term sensory. The account will prioritise smell, as does the rest of this volume, but will also examine dialectal encodings of the other senses, so that a full range of dialect can be examined.

Black Country Dialect—A Short History

Dialect writing has been problematic since the rise of a standard language across the English-speaking world. With the rise of print media and the advent of the nation state in the seventeenth century, dialects associated with region began to be downgraded on a national level. Milroy[5] explains that standardisation can be enforced more effectively at the written level:

> [S]tandardisation inhibits linguistic change and variability. Changes in progress tend to be resisted until they have spread so widely that the written and public media have to accept them. Even in the highly standardised areas of English spelling and punctuation, some changes have been slowly accepted in the last thirty years. For example, in textbooks used in English composition classes around 1960, the spelling all right

was required, and alright (on the analogy of already) was an 'error'. [This change] had taken place in some usages before standard written practice accepted [it]. Standardisation inhibits linguistic change, but it does not prevent it totally: there is a constant tension between the forces of language maintenance and the acceptance of change. Thus, to borrow a term from Edward Sapir, standardisation 'leaks'. In historical interpretation it is necessary to bear in mind this slow acceptance of change into the written language in particular, because even when the written forms are not fully standardised, they are still less variable than speech is. Changes arising in speech communities may thus have been current for long periods before they appeared in written texts.

The Black Country itself was not a cohesive area and was not recognised nationally, so that in contrast with Northumberland and Lancashire, for example, work is not emerging from the region labelled as 'Black Country dialect' until the late eighteenth century.[6] By the time this does start to happen, the notion of a standard variety taught in universities, schools and mediated through the judiciary, courts and print media is well entrenched. This means that spoken dialect becomes largely the preserve of the working class and any written dialect gathered is sparse indeed. That said, there are literary sources and linguistic sources we can consider when examining language which represents the senses. The next paragraphs will provide a short background to each of these sources.

Wright's English Dialect Dictionary was published between 1898 and 1905 by Oxford University Press as an output of the work of the English Dialect Society. It has had a new lease of life in the last few years as Professor Manfred Markus of the University of Innsbruck oversaw its digitisation. It drew heavily on the work of Alexander Ellis who in 1889 had published a survey of English Dialects. It also drew on original data collected from informants by other members of the English Dialect Society (for the purposes of this volume, the collection by Georgina Frederica Jackson in Shropshire [1879] and George Northall's *Warwickshire Word Book* [1896] are some of the nearest sources). Despite accusations that Wright criticised Ellis but replicated his methods of data collection, the *EDD* produces much of great worth and can be used to investigate the meaning of words across time with some success.

In the 1950s, Harold Orton and Joseph Wright at the University of Leeds rolled out plans for a comprehensive dialect survey of England and the Isle of Man. They sent trained fieldworkers to locations across these two countries, dividing up the area into grids. For the purposes of tracking Black Country dialect, the Survey is not ideal, since it wanted to find pure, rural speech and eschewed the speech of urban residents (viewing the Black Country as urban). Nevertheless, data collected from two speakers living in Himley add to the picture we can paint of dialect in the region across time and the kinds of words that were used to discuss sensory perceptions.

The final source that was constructed deliberately to gather data about the Black Country dialect and its speakers is the *BBC Voices* survey which was conducted between 2005 and 2007.[7] Under the auspices of the University of Leeds and the BBC, teams of journalists across the UK gathered variation in Irish, Welsh, Scottish Gaelic and English. My own doctoral fieldwork was a part of this, and interviewed many residents of the Black Country, whose words for the senses I draw on here. The data collection method was unusual in that it sought to flip the interview situation and give power to the speakers of each language variety, who informed the journalists about the language they spoke on an everyday basis. A scanned interview network sheet can be seen in Fig. 10.1.

The survey itself drew explicitly on cognitive approaches to language, and Aitchison's idea that people have connections between words which form a lexical web. The Sense Relation Networks which the survey employed drew on this as a way of stimulating conversation with the fieldworkers and journalists interviewing speakers, and as a way of making sure that some power went to those being interviewed because they would have completed paper copies of the networks prior to interview. The team responsible for constructing the networks had realised the wisdom in Aitchison's work and drew on antonyms and lexical relations to form three webs—being, saying and doing, everyday life and people, places and things.

In addition to these linguistic sources which concentrate on the spoken usage of residents of the area, we can examine dialect in writing. For this I will examine poems and novels written across the nineteenth century and into the twentieth, including both published and

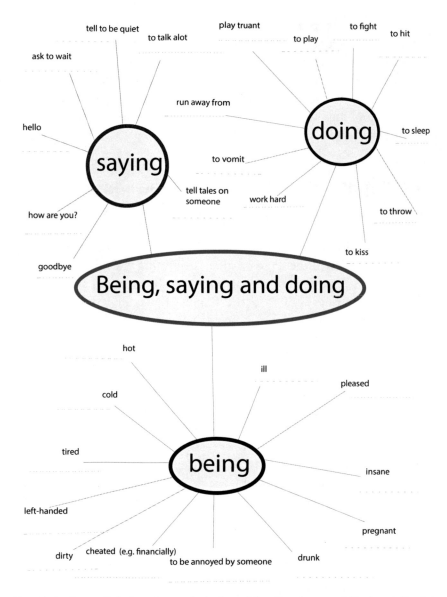

Fig. 10.1 Sense Relation Network designed for the Survey of Regional English

well-known writers and unpublished amateur writers who contribute to online poetry fora, self-published collections and local newspapers. This is important to ensure that the remains of a non-standard writing community represent what we know about the language of the senses. Middle-class writers who never spoke dialect as a first variety or who use dialect as a tool only to give flavour to literature are not as representative of the spoken language culture itself.

Black Country Dialect Lexis and the Senses up Close

I now turn to closer analysis of terms recorded in the Black Country area for things which assail the sense of smell, beginning with the term *reasty*.

Reasty has a long history of use, and can be found in the Concise Oxford Dictionary as well as in the English Dialect Dictionary. It was found in general dialectal use across England, from Cumberland to Somerset. In both the OED and EDD its primary meaning was bacon which had been poorly cured and subsequently did not keep well. The EDD explains[8]: Rancid; esp. used of bacon which has become yellow and strong-tasting through bad curing.

Examples in the EDD from Ellis's earlier dialect survey of the British Isles produce a Worcestershire speaker who explains: 'It's a bad kitchen fur keepin' bacon – it al'ays gwuz raisty – the sailin's low, an' nod much ar in it'. The EDD also lists a noun *reast* meaning bad bacon rind, and an abstract noun reastiness to describe the general process. We can also see the negative meaning attached by looking at the other adjectives *reasty* keeps company with:

It may goa maaldy or reizdy. (Yorkshire)

Dun you call this bacon? It's nasty reasty stuff. (Cheshire)

Its other listed meanings include *reasty cropped* for someone who has a sore throat, and bad tempered, as in the citation from West Yorkshire:

It woddent pay to turn reesty.

It was given by many of the people I interviewed in 2006 as an alternative for dirty in the sense of lacking personal hygiene:

> A word I would use is reasty. Reasty reasty REASTY. There's a chap who used to come here used to work at our place we used to call him reasty Roy.

This semantic shift was foreshadowed in the uses we have seen in the English Dialect Dictionary. Since unauthorised slaughter was prohibited in the Slaughter of Animals Act 1933,[9] keeping pigs at home dropped in popularity and curing one's own bacon is now not a regular occurrence in the Black Country. The shift of *reasty* to mean any food that is bad or any person that smells bad has preserved the word in the area. The same informant demonstrated how remembering one word can prime remembering another as he declared:

> Another word which I can think of for that now that's just sprung to mind is ronky. I would use that cos I called him ronky Roy all the chaps at work called him reasty Roy.

Ronk is listed in the EDD as a variant of standard *rank* (Black Country dialect often has an <o> sound before nasal consonants because it is a West Midlands dialect, so that *sond, hond and lond* as well as *bonk* for *bank* are still known in the region). It is listed as occurring from Yorkshire through Cheshire, Derbyshire, Worcestershire, Shropshire and Warwickshire down to Somerset again. Interestingly, the experience of something unpleasant is again linked to excess with a positive referent. The primary meaning of *rank* in the EDD is 'strong, great, formidable'.

My informants from Tipton, who were both 35, gave both the dirty meaning and the meaning 'great' as they discussed the meaning of the word[10]:

EA   What would you say for *dirty*?
INF 16 I can't really think of one that is particular to the area

INF 21   ronk
INF 16   Ronk yeah
INF 21   It can mean good as well though(.)I sin a band last
          night(.)oh(.)ronk band

The reported variants from the English Dialect Dictionary, the Survey of English Dialects and my own work show clearly that notions of sight, smell, touch, taste and hearing overlap. Bacon which tasted unpleasant also smelled unpleasant and gave rise to words concerning the smell of people. Smells which were unpleasant are also noted as extreme, and extremes can have an intensifying effect, as we see in the case of 'rank' (consider the intensifying use of rank in the phrase 'rank arrogance'). Winter[11] also discusses this, remarking that smell and taste in particular overlap and feed into each other, remarking that

> [t]he sensory modalities of taste and smell [...] warrant special attention: The folk model distinguishes these two senses, attributing the perception of flavor to the mouth and the tongue, even though flavor in fact arises from the interaction of taste and smell [...]

However, when the terms 'taste' and 'smell' (and correspondingly 'gustatory' and 'olfactory') are used in this book, the Aristotelian model is implied. Distinguishing taste and smell, at least initially, allows us to explore the relation between these two sensory modalities. It is interesting to see the overlap for Black Country speakers which may occur between taste and smell. The next step is to examine visual perception, and it is to this that we now turn.

While the people I interviewed for *BBC Voices* were not asked about verbs for seeing and perceiving, they were asked about adjectives to describe pleasant and unpleasant sights. Their exuberant range of phrases provides us with insight into how regional variation may persist. The keyword 'unattractive' garnered a large response which contained a wealth of dialect variation. Informants from Bilston gave 'god ugly', showing the use of 'god' as an intensifier in the Black Country (it is used as *very* would be in Standard English. Younger informants gave *minging* and *minger*, a clear borrowing from Northern and Scottish English. Its rise in English English is now waning, but it is known by most people in England now, though as the National Dictionary of Scots [NSD] explains, it has its origin again in unpleasant smells. A 1988 citation from literature describes the tell-tale smell of linoleum production in Kirkcaldy: ' ... a body wud caa out — "Neist stop Kirkcaldy" — but ye aye kent it wis Kirkcaldy oniewey on account o the ming frae the lino factories. ... '[12]

The same literary source shows how the company a word keeps can lead to meaning shift:

> The saicont ane had a pock o chips, aa reikie an mingin wi vinegar, an whan he had a chip he aye passed the pock tae ae side an tither, for his friens tae get their chips likewise.[13]

By 1994 Irvine Welsh is using the word in his Edinburgh fiction in a more generalised sense to indicate a disgusting house:

> Wi aw used tae hing aroond John Deaf's hoose. It wis really mingin likesay, but that nivir bothered ye sae much in they days.[14]

Again the notion of senses at excess is captured in the secondary meaning of minging as very drunk from 2001: While Ford gives it absolute laldy on some of his best-loved big band numbers on his album, Swing When You're Mingin'. He said: "It's usually when Scots are minging drunk that they stick a Sinatra album on and sing along — so I thought it was a great title for my album."[15]

Its use for pejoratively rating someone's attractiveness is thus clearly tied to intensifying and negatively evaluating, but the first use of this sense recorded in writing is not given in the NSD, though the OED has:

> 1985 M. MUNRO *Patter* 46 *Mingin* means stinking but can also be used to describe anything bad: 'We just came hame early cause the weather was mingin.'[16]

The NSD gives a citation from 1997 evaluating clothing which shows the move from more general negative evaluation to personal evaluation:

And the moment he came on, I thought Oh NOOOOO!! Because he was wearing the most hideous tie in the whole entire world. It was totally mingin'. It looked like something you'd buy from Oxfam for 50p to wear to a 70s night.[17]

In this way we see how an item from far away can come to be localised, and are reminded that dialect may find other ways to remain vital even as older more tightly knit community structures loosen.

'Like a Bulldog Chewing a Wasp': Is Dialect Diversity Narrowing?

Linguistic diversity around the world is under threat, with Nettle and Romaine[18] reporting:

Over the last 500 years, small languages nearly everywhere have come under intense threat. Speakers of large languages like English and Chinese find it difficult to imagine the prospect of being the last speaker of their language, but the last speakers of probably half the world's languages are alive today. Only two fluent speakers remain of the Warrwa language traditionally spoken in the Derby region of West Kimberley in Western Australia. Only about half a dozen elderly people on the island of Erromango in southern Vanuatu can still speak Ura. Marie Smith Jones is the last person who still speaks Eyak, one of Alaska's 20 some native languages. Only two (Siberian Yup'ik in two villages on St. Lawrence Island, and Central Yup'ik in 17 villages in southwestern Alaska) are spoken by children as the first language of the home. Tefvik Esenc, believed to be the last known speaker of the Ubykh language once spoken in the northwestern Caucasus, died in Turkey in 1992. The disappearance of Ubykh is the final result of a genocide of the Ubykh people, who until 1864 lived along the eastern shore of the Black Sea in the area of Sochi (northwest of Abkhazia). The entire Ubykh population left its homeland when Russia conquered the Muslim northern Caucasus in the 1860s. Tens (and possibly hundreds) of thousands of people were expelled and had to flee to Turkey with heavy loss of life, and the survivors were scattered over

Turkey. And Turkey itself is a country that until recently recognized no minorities and prohibited languages such as Kurdish from public use.

Nettle and Romaine are discussing language loss, but this loss of language might just as well be loss of dialect, since the boundaries between dialect and language are not clear to linguists. A clear example of this is the loss of status suffered by Scots after the Union of the Crowns in 1707. What had previously been referred to as *Scottis* was now supplanted gradually among the monarchy and the court, and eventually in the education system, by southern Standard English, and Scots is seen by many today as a dialect rather than a language, Nevertheless the factors that lead to dialect loss parallel those leading to language loss in many ways. Thus, David Britain[19] has commented on dialect attrition across the UK:

> I [...] make three claims in particular: firstly, that dialect death is inextricably linked to dialect contact — in order to understand how dialect death has changed the dialectological landscape of England, we need to appreciate the linguistic consequences of contact more generally; secondly, and apparently in contrast with some other speech communities, the attrition process has *not* led to a widespread shift toward RP or standard English. I argue, thirdly, that while some dialects are undoubtedly undergoing attrition, new varieties are emerging, driven by both expansion and relocation diffusion, and shaped by contact between local, regional, interregional, and other, including standard, varieties. Although the developments currently affecting English dialects in England are not necessarily particularly new, they are proceeding on an unprecedented spatial scale, a scale that has resulted from some rather wide-ranging social and economic developments that have accelerated contact between speakers of structurally distinct dialects.

Dialect attrition, that is, the loss of distinct words, pronunciations and grammatical structures which mark out dialects as different from each other, is something that concerns speech communities. Dialect speakers I interviewed often worried that younger speakers did not understand the old Black Country words. It was true that industrial dialect words like 'tundish' for a funnel were declining, and younger people often used the standard word instead. Speakers in the Black Country, though, showed that they were resilient, and gave other phrases for being unattractive that preserve linguistic richness and encompass new developments, so although more localised dialect terms are indeed being lost, identity seems to be preserved in speech using sounds and cultural experiences, albeit on a less localised level:

> face like the back end of a bus
> face like a bulldog chewing a wasp
> face like a ripped cinema sate

The examples given by my speakers interviewed in the Noughties are clear in their imagery. The simile of a rear view of a bus is not meant to be flattering, and is clearly meant to offend, or to be used outside its referent's hearing. Similarly, the image of a bulldog with its wrinkly face trying to eat a stinging insect is equally humorous and offensive. The third simile is newer, and clear to all UK cinema goers. Furry cinema seats which have been vandalised often have stuffing bursting out of them. The image created is humorous and relevant to all speakers. In addition, while image of the dog with a wasp is UK wide, the unrounded vowel which makes *wasp* rhyme with *hasp* is peculiar to the Black Country. Buses and cinemas are modern but have made their way into the idiom of the region and beyond.

Linguistic Encoding of the Senses and Emotions

In the BBC Voices study, informants reported words for emotions relating to their feelings. A sense of fright or fear would lead to crying, which many report as blarting. An anonymous poet from Walsall also used this word in a poem concerning a dog and a row with his father about walking past the dog[20]:

> Now me dad wor' avin' non o' it, cus e' knew me e' wus me dad!
> The od'e lady nex' dower, ad tode im o' wus a liy'a, un ar' wus bad.

He grabbed me by the earhole, un slung me cross his lap, e' pulled me trousers round me knees, un gid me but a slap,

Now wen od' finished blartin, o' wiped the tears from me eyses,

un O' wus snivellin in the gardin' shed, plottin' the dogs demize,

now o' could'nt use the prop, cus it wus broke, as ya' know,
so o' searched round the gardin',lookin fer summat t' throw,

Blarting is a word from Old English *blēotan*, to bleat, cry, and is ultimately related to Standard English *bleat*, The OED gives the following etymology:

1. Of sheep and cattle: to bleat, low, bellow. (See *Eng. Dial. Dict.*)
2. Of a child, etc.: to cry, whimper, howl. Also quasi-*transitive*.
    1824 W. CARR *Horæ Momenta Cravenæ* 59 *Blaat, Blate*, To bleat.
    1896 G. F. NORTHALL *Warwickshire Word-bk.* 30 *Blart*, to cry or holloa vociferously.
    1898 *Eng. Dial. Dict.* I. 289/1 He was blartin away for all the world like a babby.
    1976 A. HILL *Summer's End* ii. 30 A very young kid..blarting its eyes out.
    1976 A. HILL *Summer's End* vi. 88 He went home blarting.

The references the OED gives are all West Midlands, and the citation from Archie Hall's novel *Summer's End*[21] both places the word as Black Country and gives the restricted sense in which it is used; that is, that children *blart*. Professor Carl Chinn (Clark and Asprey 2013) reminds us that in using this verb we share a usage with Birmingham, remarking that

My nan would never say 'crying, you know, if I go to Castle Vale or Shard End the kids understand what I mean if I say pack up your blarting....

Readers of fiction concerning the Black Country that draws on dialect only for characterisation, rather than for its narration, are often presented with a sensory picture of the region which emphasises hunger, pollution, illness and discomfort. A passage from Christie Murray's novel *A Capful O' Nails*[22] is indicative:

> We lived opposite the brick kilns, and the air was always heavy with smoke and the sickening smell of burning clay. I do not know if the baking of bricks everywhere creates such a stench as it did there. Perhaps there was some peculiar quality in the clay of that district, but the odour was frightful, and wayfarers passing the brick kilns would run for a hundred yards, pinching their noses with thumb and forefinger. I have known strangers to be absolutely sickened in passing, but we who lived there were accustomed to the abominable air, and paid no heed to it, though I think that it had something to do with our general ill-health and stunted growth.

It is even the case that those whose childhood was spent as dialect speakers recall this pollution and the attendant smells well, but a rendering of these in dialect is rare. Hill (1971: 140)[23] describes Pensnett between the wars:

> The back-end of Pensnett wasn't at all good to look at. It was old and musty and there didn't seem any happiness there at all. [...] When I'd once walked this road with Gyp, he said the place was a sheer palace to what it used to be, when it was a nail making centre. I tried to tell Noggie about it like Gyp had told me, but my words didn't have the same colour about them that Gyp's did. Gyp said there used to be a nasty stench round all these houses, like an invisible shawl lapped round. Smell of urine—piss, he called it – and open sewers, smell of sulphur from the iron nail making and a thick menace of smoke from the forge-fires. Black smoke always hiding the sun.

In contrast, many present day poems looking *back* at life within the community spend less time discussing this and more discussing pleasant sensations, as we see in this discussion of drinking beer and eating dinner among Cradley chain makers from local poet Hackett[24]:

> They'd cum from the chain shaps, just up the street,
> Jones 'n Lloyds booth bottom and top,
> They'd a toil'd frum five afore it wus light,

Straight on till twelve when they'd stop.
Breakfus' time when they'd scoffed t' snap
Bout terriers 'n tumblers [racing pigeons] they'd bicker
They're peesen 'n bread was wedging thick
All dipped and drippen wi' licker.

It must be said though that some chroniclers are more reflective and possibly more honest about their sensory experiences in the region. The West Bromwich born poet Madge Gilbey[25] extracts wry humour from her memory of the taste of leftover stew, aware as she was even at the time that the stew was made from meat over a week old:

A full plert woz put daern in front ov ya
It looked like sumone ad bin sick
Tertus an mate in grey lookin werta
Wth lumps of grase floatin on it.

It ad this one gud thing gooin fer it.
Er cud mek great dumplings could mom.
An so ard ate them an leave all the rest
Ter goo back in the pot it cum from.

The appearance and reality of the food is also brought home in her hilarious tale of a young wife in Carter's Green cooking sheep's head broth for the first time, unaware that a butcher will prepare a sheep's head, cutting it in half and removing brains and jaw bone.[26]

Er kept on lookin at it but er day like what er sin. The werta wuz grey and the sheep's yed still 'ad green teeth an naer that woz all er could see in the pon. These green teeth shinin in the werta. When Fred cum um er woz sittin cryin ere art aert. It took Fred ergis tew get the story from Joyce. He went tew ave a look in the kitchin. Tekin the lid off the pon he said 'what's this Joyce, day the butcha ask ya if yow wanted it chopped in 'alf? [..]' 'E day tell me, all e said woz cook it fa three tew four hours.' [...] 'Ar bet e day tell ya tew tek the brerns aert neither did 'e?'
'Naer e day'
'Well it dow look like this when mutha cooks it.' Fred said as e started tew loff. That's when aer Joyce lost er tempa., er took the pon off the

stove an' opened the kitchen doowa. Daern the gardin 'er went an 'er swung the pon raernd then let all the dinna goo up the gardin wall.

Jon and Michael Raven's first collection of folk songs similarly includes a comic snatch of verse collected from Tettenhall concerning this dish[27]:

> Come all yew blaids whats married and yew shun hear
> A tale of what befell poor Jimmy Vight he died last night
> He never died afore. For he ate some ships yed broth
> And he did fall stiff stark stone jed under the table.

Again we see that contrary to the narrative of the honest working man making the most of his pennies, and enjoying home cooking of the cheapest cuts of meat and offal, offal dishes were a subject of ridicule, and the disgust occasioned by having to eat them was not confined to those of us who are no longer forced to. The humour in the rhyme is signalled clearly ('he never died afore') and the source of Jimmy Vight's death is said to be the sheep's head broth he has eaten.

Conclusion

Literature, dictionaries and interviews conducted with first language speakers of Black Country dialect examined in this chapter sometimes contains the lexis identified in dialect surveys by speakers as being lexis typical of the Black Country dialect to represent emotions and senses, but even when the senses and their reactions to stimuli are represented using lexis we might describe as Standard, it is clear that pollution, deprivation, and poverty as well as hunger and thirst are often topics discussed. Given the industrial heritage of the Black Country and the lack of any regulations concerning pollution, sewerage or working hours during the first stages of the Industrial Revolution, this is perhaps not a surprise.

We can see that the senses of smell and taste are indeed tightly linked and often one feeds into the representation of the other over time. It also seems possible that humour is used across the ages to blot out the memories of having to eat poor and unpalatable food, and that a more sanitised approach to the assault on the sight, smell and taste which living in the

Black Country represented is only possible at arm's length or through the distance imposed by time.

Gilbey, moreover, sees a change in the region and a return to health and even pleasant sights[28]:

> When I see the playing fields in the morning
> With the sun bejewelled grass
> I think to myself
> What Black Country?
>   It doesn't make any sense
>   To call it that.
>
> When I see the hedge's multi-coloured leaves
> And the birds playing in their branches
> I think to myself
> How Black Country
>   The blackness isn't there
>   It's gone at last.
>
> When I am walking around the garden at dawn
> The dew dropping from the flowers
> I think to myself
> Dead Black Country
>   Leaving behind greenness
>   To be enjoyed.

In some respects, the removal of decay and smells from the region is bitterly ironic since the pollution signalled employment as well as danger and illness. The idea that heavy industry and its loss can be mourned even as it leads to lower air pollution and a better quality of health is anathema to some, but captured perfectly by writers like Anthony Cartwright and Archie Hill. It is also clear that even among individual writers and speakers, life in the Black Country is far from pleasant at times even now, and that while they may have a close sensory bond with the place they come from, they are acutely aware of its shortcomings and the problems it still has. Continuing descriptions of unemployment, loss of self esteem, poor self image in the eyes of the UK and a loss of green space and physical beauty in the region abound. For the residents who speak it and write in it, their dialect remains a spoken and written possibility for capturing the illness, bad smells and bad tastes that life in the Black Country continues to throw up. As Britain argued,[29] their dialect is changing but it is by no means dead, and in fact has been enriched through contact and enriched by the new experiences speakers in the modern Black Country region have had, taking in the modern comforts of public transport and cinema, and the possibility of refrigerators to prevent mouldy and decaying food. It will be instructive to watch the speech community as they discuss these changes to the place where they live and put down their renderings of sensation on paper.

Notes

1. A. Cartwright, *Heartland* (Birmingham: Tindall Street Press, 2009).
2. Ministry of Housing, Communities and Local Government. 'The English Indices of Deprivation 2019', September 2019. https://assets.publishing. service.gov.uk/government/uploads/system/uploads/attachment_data/file/ 835115/IoD2019_Statistical_Release.pdf.
3. Nik Coupland and Hywel Bishop. 'Ideologised Values for British Accents', *Journal of Sociolinguistics* 11, no. 1 (2007): 74–93.
4. Bodo Winter, *Sensory Linguistics: Language, Perception and Metaphor* (Amsterdam: John Benjamins Publishing Company, 2019), 12–13.
5. J. Milroy, 'Historical Description and the Ideology of the Standard Language', in *The Development of Standard English, 1300–1800 Theories, Descriptions, Conflicts*, edited by Laura Wright (Cambridge: Cambridge University Press).
6. Esther Asprey, 'Black Country Dialect Literature and What It Can Tell Us About Black Country Dialect', in *Dialect Writing and the North of England*, edited by Patrick Honeybone and Warren Maguire (Edinburgh: Edinburgh University Press, in press), 29–50.
7. BBC Voices project, 'Where I Live', 2013 http://www.bbc.co.uk/blackc ountry/voices/intro.shtml.
8. *English Dialect Dictionary online*, 9 February 2019. http://eddonline-proj. uibk.ac.at/edd/index.jsp.
9. Question to the House, 21 December 1933, relating to the Slaughter of Animals Act. https://api.parliament.uk/historic-hansard/commons/1933/ dec/21/slaughter-of-animals-act-1933.

10. Esther Asprey, 'Black Country English and Black Country Identity', Unpublished doctoral thesis. Leeds: University of Leeds, 2007.
11. Winter, Bodo. *Sensory Linguistics: Language, Perception and Metaphor* (Amsterdam: John Benjamins Publishing Company, 2019), 12.
12. Dictionary of the Scots Language entry for 'ming'. https://dsl.ac.uk/entry/snd/sndns2554.
13. Dictionary of the Scots Language entry for 'ming'. https://dsl.ac.uk/entry/snd/sndns2554.
14. Dictionary of the Scots Language entry for 'ming'. https://dsl.ac.uk/entry/snd/sndns2554.
15. Dictionary of the Scots Language entry for 'ming'. https://dsl.ac.uk/entry/snd/sndns2554.
16. *Oxford English Dictionary online*, 'minging'. https://0-www-oed-com.pug wash.lib.warwick.ac.uk/view/Entry/245656?isAdvanced=false&result=6& rskey=J9sjxp.
17. Dictionary of the Scots Language entry for 'ming' https://dsl.ac.uk/entry/snd/sndns2554.
18. Daniel Nettle and Suzanne Romaine, *Vanishing Voices: The Extinction of the World's Languages* (Oxford: Oxford University Press, 2000).
19. Dave Britain, 'One Foot in the Grave? Dialect Death, Dialect Contact, and Dialect Birth in England', *International Journal of the Sociology of Language* (2009): 196–197.
20. Peter Bounce. 'Nex Dower's Dog', 2014. Available at http://www.bbc.co.uk/blackcountry/features/2002/12/accents/black_country_stories_and_poems1.shtml. Accessed on 14 January 2020.
21. Archie Hill, *Summer's End* (London: Sheapherd Walwyn, 1976).
22. David Christie Murray, *A Capful O' Nails* (London: Chatto and Windus, 1896), 6.
23. Archie Hill, *Summer's End* (London: Sheapherd Walwyn, 1976).
24. Glenys Hackett, 'The Chainmakers', in *Cradley Then and Now* (Cradley, West Midlands, s.n., s.d).
25. Madge Gilbey, *Moowa Poems and Stories from the Black Country Wench* (Oldbury: Transform Sandwell Printing Services, s.d.), 19.
26. Madge Gilbey, *Moowa Poems and Stories from the Black Country Wench* (Oldbury: Transform Sandwell Printing Services, s.d.), 21.
27. Michael Raven and Jon Raven, *Folksongs of the Black Country* (Wolverhampton: Wolverhampton Folk Song Club, 1964).
28. Madge Gilbey, *Moowa Poems and Stories from the Black Country Wench* (Oldbury: Transform Sandwell Printing Services, s.d.), 42.

29. Dave Britain, 'One Foot in the Grave? Dialect Death, Dialect Contact, and Dialect Birth in England', *International Journal of the Sociology of Language* (2009): 196–197.

Works Cited

Asprey, Esther. 'Black Country English and Black Country Identity', Unpublished doctoral thesis. Leeds: University of Leeds. 2007.

Asprey, Esther. 'Black Country Dialect Literature and What It Can Tell Us About Black Country dialect', in *Dialect Writing and the North of England*, edited by Patrick Honeybone and Warren Maguire (Edinburgh: Edinburgh University Press, in press), 29–50.

Britain, David. 'One Foot in the grave? Dialect Death, Dialect Contact, and Dialect Birth in England', *International Journal of the Sociology of Language* (2009): 121–155, 196–197. https://doi.org/10.1515/IJSL.2009.019.

Cartwright, A. *Heartland* (Birmingham: Tindall Street Press, 2009).

Clark, Urszula and Esther Asprey. *West Midlands English: Birmingham and the Black Country* (Edinburgh: Edinburgh University Press, 2013).

Coupland, Nik and Hywel Bishop. 'Ideologised Values for British Accents', *Journal of Sociolinguistics* 11, no. 1 (2007): 74–93. https://doi.org/10.1111/j.1467-9841.2007.00311.x.

Dictionary of the Scots Language. https://dsl.ac.uk/.

Gilbey, Madge. *Moowa Poems and Stories from the Black Country Wench* (Oldbury: Transform Sandwell Printing Services, s.d. [XXXX]).

Hackett, J. 'Tymes Gon Bye', in *Cradley Poems and Dialect Words*, edited by Jill Guest (Cradley Heath: Leopard Press, 2011).

Markus, Manfred (ed). Innsbruck EDD Online 3.0 (based on Joseph Wright's *English Dialect Dictionary, 1898–1905*). http://eddonline-proj.uibk.ac.at/edd/termsOfUse.jsp.

Ministry of Housing, Communities and Local Government. 'The English Indices of Deprivation 2019', September 2019. https://assets.publishing.service.gov.uk/government/uploads/system/uploads/attachment_data/file/835115/IoD2019_Statistical_Release.pdf.

Nettle, Daniel and Suzanne Romaine. *Vanishing Voices: The Extinction of the World's Languages* (Oxford: Oxford University Press, 2000).

Orton, H. and M. Barry (eds). *Survey of English Dialects (B): The Basic Material—Volume 2 Part 1—The West Midland Counties* (Leeds: E.J. Arnold. 1969).

Orton, H. and M. Barry (eds). *Survey of English Dialects (B): The Basic Material—Volume 2 Part 2—The West Midland Counties* (Leeds: E.J. Arnold,. 1970).

Orton, H., and M. Barry (eds). *Survey of English Dialects (B): The Basic Material—Volume 2 Part 3—The West Midland Counties* (Leeds: E.J. Arnold. 1971).

Oxford English Dictionary. 2nd ed. 20 vols (Oxford: Oxford University Press, 1989). Continually updated at http://www.oed.com/.

Raven, Michael and Jon Raven. *Folksongs of the Black Country* (Wolverhampton: Wolverhampton Folk Song Club, 1964).

Winter, Bodo. *Sensory Linguistics: Language, Perception and Metaphor* (Amsterdam: John Benjamins Publishing Company, 2019).

Wright, Joseph. *The English Dialect Dictionary, Being the Complete Vocabulary of All Dialect Words Still in Use, or Known to Have Been in Use During the Last Two Hundred Years; Founded on the Publications of the English Dialect Society and on a Large Amount of Material Never Before Printed* (London: Oxford University Press, 1898–1905).

11

Goo An' Fetch the Tundish

Brendan Hawthorne

When a chill gripped the house
away from the coal-filled hearth
he'd put on his overcoat
tilt his trilby
knot his muffler
put a few of bob in his trouser pocket
and carry the empty gallon Jerrys
up to the hardware store
He'd allus fetch blue
Never pink
Blue burned clean
blue was expensive
Pink smoked
but was cheap
And when he got back

B. Hawthorne (✉)
Wednesbury, UK

© The Author(s), under exclusive license to Springer
Nature Switzerland AG 2021
S. Groes et al. (eds.), *Smell, Memory, and Literature in the Black Country*,
https://doi.org/10.1007/978-3-030-57212-9_11

the familiar smell of paraffin
pervaded the house with
domesticated gas oil tang
He'd say 'Goo an fetch the tundish, me lad!'
He'd place his snipped nub end Park Drive fag down
on top of the powder coated case
and then as a kid
I'd follow him around the house
topping up the Valor heaters
with the glug glug glug through
the time-faded tundish
'Doe sheed it' he'd say
and with expert eye
and steady hand
he'd dispense the cobalt coloured liquid
that glistened like sapphires
In the half light
I'd watch the diamond shaped crystals
turn from clear to black
from empty to full
on the filler tank
We'd allus start in the veranda
then the sitting room
and after a careful trim
the wicks would be set
ready to ignite into that
dancing blue ring of heat
With a spark and a touch
of the sulphurous brimstone strike
the glass would be brought
down slowly to rest
careful not to tilt
the spring on the snuffer
He'd close the bright orange door
and heat would satisfactorily
drift from the vents
He'd then store the cans
in the back privy
the tundish wiped free of residue

and placed over the cap
of one of the cans
And I'd feel cosy and warm
between the heat of coal
and the smell of paraffin
And several years later when he'd gone
and I had to sort a few things out
in the cold light of day
I noticed that he'd left enough fuel
in those Jerrys
to top up those heaters once more
The tundish remained placed to the side
and I knew what I had to do
When I heard him say in my memory
'Goo an fetch the tundish, lad
Doe sheed it
Careful with the snuffer
Get the trimmer. Yo'll need it'
and as the smell of blue paraffin
fuelled my senses
I realised that the ritual
after all these years
had been passed on
from him
to me.

12

Bella

R. M. Francis

It's hard to be clear when you're dead. Nothing holds in the same way. It's hard. I recall the smell of pig shit and how it slugs at my throat. When I lived I could get that smell in a mood. When the mood was right, I could smell it and every organ in me would flex and shiver. When there was a bad mood. That rank stench and body quiver – I'll never know where it came from or how it mustered so much feeling. That's what it's like now. My life is held in rushes of smells and the moods that flood with each sniff. Memory is difficult when you're dead.

Mom married Dad when I was still inside her. He worked days and she worked nights, so it was me and Nan. Me and Nan pulled potatoes in the field. She made the best chips around. Potatoes and pig shit. Sweat and soil. You would gag on it, and like the gag too, sometimes. I learned to like Dad's belt too, sometimes. Mom normally liked it for me. There's no pain out here

R. M. Francis (✉)
University of Wolverhampton, Wolverhampton, UK

in the woods. Just the spasms of smelling things. Memory is difficult and these spasms are like tears – they soothe and soil.

Dad had one leg. They cut it off in the trench. That cut saved the rest of him. He screams sometimes, he can still feel it. That's what you do too. When you wander in to Saltwells looking for the Wych-Elm, chasing rumours and that empty stomach feeling, you find the bit they cut away. You call me Bella.

Memory is difficult but I see like cut crystal. I see you when you wander in. That brown skinned boy, he is terrified. Skinny limbs shivering. Sweat pearled over flesh. Deep brown eyes bold and wide. He breathes in gasps through a wide mouth. I don't know if he saw me but he froze. He froze at the Wych-Elm. Just stared. Stared straight through me. He was stiff. Then he collapses – slumped at the trunk. I stood and looked over him. I took in every pore of him. Then those older guys came and grabbed him and pulled him away. The oldest was strong. The oldest seemed to know more. He could see something of me. He said, Doh look, doh look at 'er. They carried him away in a rush.

I can't piece it together. Can't fully make a picture from these senses. I said it was like a smell. Like the smell that electrifies through the body. The incense at St Andrew's on a Sunday. Dad's beer breath. Mom's carbolic soap. I taste it and I don't know if I should relish in it. It sits just out of view – a blurred spot in the corner of your eye – and every time you turn to see it, it's gone. You don't know if it's a devil or a guardian. That's how it is.

You step into the woods and you step away from the path. That's when you start to notice. Away from the normal routes the things you hear become more, and it becomes more for you that you can't see what makes it. The fidget of animals. The insect buzz. On the path you'd shake it off, but here, with me, you can't be sure. It's a throb. The throb grows with each step closer to the Wych-Elm. Most of you turn back early. Some of you make it to the tree. Some of you see me. You call me Bella and you know I see you.

There are two boys who come to me. They come unafraid. Not totally unafraid – less so. I see them grab at each other and kiss. They rub hungry hands over each other. They bite lips and scratch at backs. I see one take a cock in his mouth and spend delicate moments sucking, licking thrusting pelvis into face. They look at each other and small smiles curl in the corner of their mouths. They stroke each other's cheek. They kiss. They kiss over and over. They are starved and each is a feast for the other.

The first time I saw them they were dancing. They'd been drinking. They took it in turns. They lay on the damp earth and cuddled. With heavy breath, sweat dripping, curled up in each other's limbs. I saw it all. At one moment they must have seen too. They must have half seen or sensed me seeing. Something startled them. They dressed and rushed off.

I like to see them. They got used to the woods. I think they got used to my stare. They come back often to love each other.

Memory is difficult but I remember feelings, smells. I think I do.

In the springtime the woods are fresh, green, wet. They are acrid, fetid. We're stuck in the muck of it all.

We were all over each other. We couldn't let each other go. Her lips, tongue, teeth against my neck, my breast. Hot breath. Panting. She pinned my arms behind my back. Face pressed into my frame. Ripped back my skirt. Circled cunt.

Memory is difficult. It's just flashes of moods.

This is when you came. We heard the snap of twigs, the muttering voices, the muted footsteps. This is when we froze. We stopped. Stared at each other, scared. You were ten strong against us. You stepped through the thicket and out into our space. Circled us.

13

The Rise of Black Countryness: Place-Identity and the Black Country

R. M. Francis

Place-Identity: A Brief Introduction

The Black Country, like many post-industrial regions in the Western world, is an off-kilter space. A space of loss, marginality, unusual and ambiguous geographies. This chapter uses Environmental Psychology to consider how place shapes our sense of self, and draws on ideas of the Uncanny, the Eerie and the Weird to investigate how off-kilter environments manifest off-kilter identities. In doing so, I claim that in the hyper-modern digital realms of our contemporary lives we require physical and sensory links to our locales in order to maintain a strong sense of place-identity.

Much work has been done in the field of environmental psychology in terms of how the formation of identity is linked to sense of place. The Environmental Psychologists call this Place-Identity. Coined by Harold Poshansky, it is defined as:

R. M. Francis (✉)
University of Wolverhampton, Wolverhampton, UK

© The Author(s), under exclusive license to Springer
Nature Switzerland AG 2021
S. Groes et al. (eds.), *Smell, Memory, and Literature in the Black Country*,
https://doi.org/10.1007/978-3-030-57212-9_13

a sub-structure of the self-identity of the person consisting of, broadly conceived, cognitions about the physical world in which the individual lives. These cognitions represent memories, ideals, feelings, attitudes, values, preferences, meanings, and conceptions of behavior and experience which relate to the variety and complexity of physical settings [...] consisting of places, spaces and their properties which have served instrumentally in the satisfaction of the person's biological, psychological, social, and cultural needs.[1]

We move through places, and in doing so attach and distance ourselves respectively, like caddisfly larvae collecting materials for their pupae, to physical locations that we imbibe with feelings, values, meanings, and importantly, memories. As Groes and Mercer points out in Chapter 7, these memories are deeply embedded in our neurological networks by sensory data—sounds, sights, tastes, smells. In short, we Snidge Scrump—Black Country slang for using your nose to forage—our route to place-identity.

Anton and Lawrence use Proshanksy's definition in their paper, using a qualitative survey to show that place-identity comes about through the fulfilment of a need or as an act of dependency:

a place meets a person's needs so they become dependent on it and choose to stay there. The longer a person stays in a place the greater the likelihood of the place being incorporated into the identity structure, especially if that place also provides the individual with feelings of distinctiveness, continuity, self-esteem and self-efficacy.[2]

The case studies and data in their paper suggest that sense of place and identity within that place comes about through dependency or functional needs that take on further psychical or emotional connections as a secondary move. This is echoed by Clarke, Murphy and Lorenzoni, who argue that 'place dependence refers to functional features of a place that facilitate certain activities and emotional connections'.[3]

In their article 'Place and Identity Process', Twiggler-Ross and Uzzell use the model that 'identity should be conceptualized in terms of a biological organism moving through time which develops through the accommodation, assimilation and evaluation of the social world'.[4]

Their argument suggests that identity is formed, in part, by a series of drives and acts that either attach or distance the subject from their environment—creating a sense of place. They argue that:

> distinctiveness summarizes a lifestyle and establishes that person as having a specific type of relationship with his/her home environment, which is clearly distinct from any other type of relationship [...] people use place identifications in order to distinguish themselves from others. In this sense place functions in a similar way to a social category and therefore place identifications can be thought of as comparable to social identifications.[5]

One's relationship with and connectedness to their hometown, their housing estate, the landmarks and histories that make up their locale, are as important to one's identity as their gender, class, race and sexuality. Rijnks and Strijker discuss this in terms of regionality:

> The basic principle of defining a region is to find a set of common characteristics, which include, but are not limited to, geographical location, physical features, socio-economic qualifications, political situations and cultural characteristics. Defining a region requires it to be distinguishable from other (neighbouring) regions, so it follows that in defining what a region is, equally we are defining what a region is not [...] Regions are defined by the characteristics they are associated with, which in turn influence the identity ascribed to that region. Equally, regions that are defined as being different to a certain region help shape the identity of this region, as characteristics attributed to the other region, but not associated with one's own, solidify the definition of one's own region.[6]

Local foods and smells are a major factor in this formation of regional identity. The Black Country smells identified in the Snidge Scrumpin' experiments as responsible for forging memory and place stand as evidence of this (see chapter 7). Rijnks and Stijker discuss how resilient regional identity is, how it is dependent on acts of othering and how important it is, for many, in sense of self. They argue, 'regional identity consists of (perceived) characteristics of a region incorporated in one's own identity'.[7] These perceived characteristics are subjective and selective on the part of the observer, but also relate to a collective or communal reflection of place too. These are built from inherited cultural memories, traditions and histories manifest in buildings, cultural figures and shared experiences of location and events.

Twigger-Ross and Uzzell break place-identity into two separate, but equally important, paths in the process: place-referent continuity and place-congruent continuity. Place-referent continuity is the idea 'that places act as referents to past selves and actions and that for some people, maintenance of a link with that place provides a sense of continuity to their identity'.[8] Place-congruent continuity 'refers to the maintenance of continuity via characteristics of places which are generic and transferable from one place to another'.[9] So, the subject defines self in relation to a place because of the place's cultural current (i.e. its unique history, artistic heritage, particular topographies/geography, one's own familial and personal memories and feelings), as well as the recognition of the place's utilitarian or convenience aspects (i.e. quality of local schools, transport links, shopping facilities). Clarke, Murphy and Lorenzoni reiterate this: 'both physical and social attributes of place are interconnected and mutually reinforce place attachment processes'.[10] Most important is the continuity of those currents. The article suggests that:

> having control, or not, over the maintenance of continuity of place is important for psychological well-being [because] unwanted and personally uncontrollable change in the physical environment, resulting in the loss of the principle of continuity, may cause a grief or loss reaction.[11]

The place-referent part of the argument is most pertinent to this topic: the cultural, historical and personalised makeup of a place that defines it as unique. Black Countryness is defined by some of the following markers—its industrial heritage, odd geography and mix of dialects set it apart from many other areas. This uniqueness of place infiltrates the communal identity of its population, acting as an important marker and/or mirror of how they see themselves in the world.

In his Jacksonville TEDxTalk, *Where Am I? The Power of Uniqueness*, Ed McMahon discusses the psychological, political and economic benefits of preserving sense of place. He argues: 'Place is more than just a spot on the map. Place is what makes your hometown different from my hometown, but more importantly, I believe, sense of place is explicitly that which makes our physical surroundings worth caring about'.[12] Using various examples of 'cared for' and 'uncared for' places, he makes a case for the ways local history and culture benefit areas, both in terms of economics and investment, and in terms of well-being and communal connection. He focuses on areas of historical significance, suggesting: 'Another thing that affects value and sense of place is the presence or absence of historic buildings and neighbourhoods [...] it's about physically connecting people to the past, it's about telling you who you are and where you came from'.[13] McMahon is talking about shared memory, communal memory, and how that aids in forging connections between individuals set in a specific location. Importantly, this argument relies on being physically and/or sensorially connected to our pasts. This echoes environmental psychology: heritage acting as an anchor for sense of place, underpinning identity. McMahon calls for the protection and conservation of the cultural and historical, not just so they remain, but so they might hold the full potential of their cultural significance. It's not good enough to have a monument to something or someone if the area around it doesn't allow for its appreciation. In terms of the Black Country then, we might ask: what good is protecting the legacy of Dudley born filmmaker, James Whale,[14] if his monument is in the middle of a car park surrounded by Pizza Hut, Nando's and McDonalds? Indeed, most people in Dudley, as well as its visitors wouldn't know where to go to see his memorial. McMahon further argues:

> It's not because we can't plant new trees and build new buildings, It's because, I believe, our sense of identity and well being is tied in a very profound way to special buildings and places and views. These places are invested with rich symbolic importance that contributes to our sense of identity and well being in a way no less fundamental than religion, our language, our culture [...] Not just about the economy of this state, it's about the psychology of this state as well.[15]

Environmental psychology and McMahon suggest that our sense of place, be it attachment or detachment, is based around a system of symbols that organise the cultural identity and demographic of place. Part of this system is the sensory information held in spaces. As pointed out in Chapter 7, our memories are anchored to smells and tastes from specific sites and times—we know our pasts, and thus our sense of self, because of this. Environmental Psychology offers further evidence of this, examining what happens to place-identity during times of social or geographical upheaval. Anton and Lawrence argue that 'threats to a place may increase people's awareness of their attachment [...] and influence them to want to stay in the place they are attached to, despite the place no longer being safe'.[16] Clarke, Murphy and Lorenzoni state that '[i]ndividuals subjected to such processes may deploy coping mechanisms (e.g. resisting change, re-establishing place meanings, questioning powerful interests) to reduce threats of disruptions and protect their sense of attachment'.[17] Place attachment, regardless of threats to safety of people, is an important marker of identity. Indeed, this sense of self within a location might even become stronger during times of upheaval or change. These studies show how things like political or environmental change impact on the culture and geography of an area, often resulting in a strengthened desire for continuity and heightened sense of place-identity. One such upheaval is the destruction of industry and rise of digital life/experience—as we move away from sensory and physical connectedness, we risk the erasure of our collective memories and sense of self within place.

The Rise of Black Countryness

The rise of Black Countryness is, in many ways a post-industrial one, celebrating what once was; the Black Country flag, Black Country Day, and arts organisations such as Creative Black Country and Multistory are all post-millennial. The University of Wolverhampton launched the Black Country Studies Centre in 2019.[18] This nostalgic or belated pride indicates the need for communities, especially post-industrial ones, to protect and maintain their regional place-identity.

There is more at play here too. This is not just maintenance and protection; it is reimagining and recreating heritage. In some ways

Black Countryness forges itself by remembering the cultural echo of its landscape. Place-identification is a structuring of selfhood set within a location, forged through communal and social influences and with more personal, subjective, imagined responses. This creates the genius-loci or the power of place.

So, what might we call the *genius loci* of the Black Country? In his book, *Dudley & Netherton Remembered*, Ned Williams makes a case for the Black Country, Dudley and then specifically Netherton, as having the unique and peculiar qualities mentioned in the introduction. He describes the various townships of the region as 'simply federations of smaller units',[19] explaining that although Dudley is the main hub of a town, it is broken into smaller suburbs/areas—each one having their own particular character. This, he argues, is born directly from the way in which local firms and industries worked and how significant their place in the community was. He suggests that, 'Chain producing works like Noah Hingley's became complete communities in themselves where everybody lived in close proximity, worked together, drank in the same pubs and worshipped in the same chapels'.[20] Williams argues two things here: that the Black Country is a strange group of interlinking areas, where the whole and the components are difficult to view in singular but somehow impossible to ignore in their separateness; and, that these individual townships that mesh to make the larger network came about through localised industry and commitment to community. Many post-industrial European places share this; what is lost, is not just the steelworks or manufacturing districts, it's the hub of communal activity that once orbited those works, and their accompanying smells— hoppy, smoke-filled pubs, church incense, forge fires. The growth of protectionist, bordered, regionalist or nationalist activity and thought throughout Europe and The West may in part be a reaction to this loss. The loss of physical connections to places and communities following the social media revolution is further evidence of this desire to uphold and maintain The Region. Williams takes his point further in 'Netherton: People and Places', saying not only is it possible to break the Black Country down into small parts, not only is it possible to break Dudley down into smaller parts, 'It is possible to continue the process by dividing Netherton into parts [like] Baptist End, Cinder Bank, Windmill End,

Primrose Hill, Lodge Hill Farm'.[21] In this book he provides an excellent description of how Netherton appears today, having faced the challenges of industrialisation and de-industrialisation:

> It is now difficult to imagine the number of small pits that covered the area during the first half of the twentieth century, or imagine the landscape through which canals were built [...] the legacy on the ground has been subsidence. Subsidence meant that much of the old Netherton had to be replaced [...] by the middle of the twentieth century Netherton was an interesting mixture of the old and the not so old. Add to that the developments that have taken place since the middle of the twentieth century and we have a very complex landscape that now forms today's Netherton [...] Can Netherton and similar Black Country towns ever be more than just dormitories in the modern conurbation?[22]

Just as Black Country dormitories sit almost dormant in the shadow of cosmopolitan Birmingham, so too do areas like London's Isle of Dogs, shadowed by Canary Wharf, or the high-rise estates of Hungary's Avas against the metropolitan Belvaros. These are overlooked and unlooked for places, slightly lost and holding tightly to their heritage, their communal memories. These are also the places where the sensory data one uses to connect oneself to their locale, have too become post-industrial; that is to say, sanitised or dulled.

Memory is precious. Especially in a post-industrial world of fake news, info-bots and newsfeed addiction. Where the homogenous high streets, retail zones and housing estates, replace and erase the past. We face our own hypermodern amnesia.

In terms of evolutionary biology, the purpose of memory is not necessarily to merely remember the past but to extract from the past that with which one needs to structure one's future. It's the once bitten, twice shy or the fool me once rules of life. Memory is pragmatic, steering us away from future risks and towards experiences that sustain. Bryson talks about this as a patchwork quilt—a weaving together of past, present and future recollections and imaginings—that one cloaks oneself in as a means of personal and social maintenance and development.[23] Memories are seldom unfixed from locations and time-spaces, the Snidge Scrumpin' experiments' results confirm this referent place-identities. If memory acts as a biological survival imperative, then so too do our collective communal recollections. This is a conservative argument at heart—tradition preserves and protects.

A significant aspect of our subjectivity is the way culture colours our worlds and our views. These cultures are entwined with the signs and stories we pass from generation to generation. I distinguish myself, in part, through the symbols that organise my culture. A major aspect of this is shared memory—the story of my grandparents' legacy of jungle combat in Malaya, the shared family memories of caravan holidays in Wales, the communal memory that my place of birth was the cradle of the industrial revolution, and the time I realised Robert Plant was stood next to me on the terraces of Lye Town Football Club—my mate's Uncle used to work the warehouse with him at Woolworths in Halesowen and he became one of the most important pop culture figures of all time. This string of memories can be summoned by the simple sniff of a cup of Bovril from a polystyrene cup, and are harnessed in the estates from where I grew up. Memories act like a cuirass, their rhizomes anchoring us to our cultures, communities and the places they haunt. Bryson's quilt of memory is part of the formation of that rootedness. Anton and Lawrence suggest that sense of place is shaped by memories, ideas, feelings and values set within a specific locale.

O'Brien has explored issues of poetry of place, looking at the various things the creative writer must balance when addressing place.[24] Although O'Brien discusses England and Englishness as a wider topic, much is still relevant in his argument. He lays out the messiness of attempting to write of a particular place and of a specific identity: 'The dead ends and false trails, are part of the imagined England in which we live'.[25] Likewise, I'd argue, are the dead ends and contradictions of the Black Country. O'Brien suggests that 'some places may seem more "England" than others'[26] and that there are inherent contradictions and difficulties in representing the local due to the interrelated contradictions in the history of a place. He uses Northumbria and Yorkshire as examples of places and identities that attempt to mark themselves out as a different kind, a potentially more authentic kind, of England: 'that making of an exception was also a claim to original authenticity, to having been in some sense here before the Normans, who are definitely "not from round here".[27] O'Brien suggests an Environmental Psychologists' view; that a community or culture mark themselves out as different from other communities, through the conservation, promotion and celebration of their shared history, language/vernacular and successes. O'Brien also argues that there are certain places that claim an 'original authenticity', which not only marks them out as particular or different, but marks them out as a linked in a pseudo-genetic way. This can be appropriated to the Black Country when one considers the region's role in the industrial revolution and its population's pride in that. It can also be considered in terms of the preoccupation with Mercian and Anglo-Saxon ancestry. A sense of pride and lineage stems from the fact that the region's dialects have their roots in the Saxon, Germanic and Mercian languages; attention is given to Wulfruna, Grand-daughter of Aethelflaed (Daughter of Alfred the Great), who gives her name to Wolverhampton. This too is a marker of exception, one that suggests a uniqueness of spirit, class, strength and a genealogical link to a 'real' 'authentic' place in the UK's history. These notions border on the essentialist and the exclusionary, begging the questions: what is authentic and who decides what qualifies? The authenticity of these claims is unimportant—part of the building blocks of place-identification are the myths and stories we tell ourselves about a locale. Indeed, as we know so little factual details of this pre-Norman Britain, as so much of the history is recorded through hearsay and Norman propaganda, it's impossible to make an authentic and rational claim about this. The Mercian heritage of the region becomes a myth; a narrative linked to a place. The sense of place is part-fact and part-fable, much like O'Brien suggests when talking about Englishness—the dead-ends and false trails play their part too. This is evident in the haunting qualities of the Black Country landscape and the off-kilter communal memories; the authentic ontology of the ghosts that contribute to the region's spirit of place is unimportant.

O'Brien continues to discuss the various contradictions and slippery aspects of Englishness, concluding that it is both open for potential and inherently weak, calling this:

> a visionary state located neither in the past, present nor future. Imaginatively this is a powerful position - that of timeless, the immanent, the

imminent, the possible - but in crudely political terms it is to the same extent vulnerable. It does not require proof, and cannot supply it.[28]

As such, one needs to be alert to this multitude of contradictions in one's views, in the history records and in the myths, but, to the same extent, open to timeless, immanent and imminent possibilities. The spirit of place and place-identity can be written as a bricolage of real and unreal, fiction and non-fiction. Yet, it must always, for the sake of self, have its rhizomes rooted in sensory soils.

Black Country writers, Paul McDonald and Anthony Cartwright explore this in their novels, where landscapes are symbolically charged with folklore, history, family memories. Like Bryson's metaphor, readers cannot distinguish the sutures between these things: Cartwright's characters are imbued in equal measure by the ghosts of the steelworks, the gangs in the housing estates, miners strikes and tales of Anglo-Saxon battles; McDonald's characters are surrounded by the sardonic and irreverent humour, born out of the ridiculous and surreal situations that face those living in nowhere towns. Their place-identity is a web of personal, familial, social and cultural memory. This place-identity becomes important to one's sense of self—providing distinctiveness, community. Our sense of place is what marks us out as an individual as well what marks us out as part of a pack. If place is such an important marker of subjecthood and sense of place is built up from the history, stories and heritage of the constantly evolving locale then memory too, in this case communal memory, is part of that protective patchwork quilt of stored narratives.

Passing down memories across generations acts as a collective call to responsibility that protects the individual and the collective. We pass down more than just bedtime stories, we pass down narratives that sustain and endure. These memories act as myths that provide a culture with a shared set of morals and attitudes, these establish themselves within a culture acting not only as foundation but also as a sense of purpose. They are the pragmatic memory tools—steering us, cloaking us.

These collective histories are and have been at risk for some time. The local high street with its family run bakers, grocers and cobblers has been usurped by twenty-four hour supermarkets and large, indoor shopping centres. Factories and building merchants are replaced by call-centres, multi-national corporations. The steel and mining industries are overtaken by recruitment agencies that offer positions in the recruitment industry. The landscape and its olfactory climate are irredeemably changed, as Stuart Connor shows in Chapter 16. We've developed what Marc Auge called 'non-places',[29] which are transient places, lacking in cultural or social significance: motorways, shopping centres, waiting rooms. In the non-place, life is lived and contemplated through screens of adverts, social media, reality TV and rolling news. Our histories are experienced through mawkish nostalgia. In this, the subject is lost, or perhaps in an ambiguous position—somewhere between terror and bliss. Fredric Jameson argued that 'in such a world, local cultures struggle to have any meaning and we all lose our sense of historical and geographical place'.[30] This hypermodernity strips away the rich cultural memory, customs and knowledges. It unpicks the patchwork of our protective quilts. It leaves us under threat of erasure—as marginal, liminal half-beings set in hypermodern non-places. These non-places are such, in part, because they are non-smelling or artificially smelling places. They are absent of memory-provoking-smells, or filled with manufactured scents, designed to make environments more conducive to shopping. A Black Country example of this Merry Hill Shopping Centre: when built, the largest shopping mall in Europe, it was one of 1980s repurposing of industrial space. The site used to belong to Roundoak Steelworks. It is easy to imagine how the spirit of place and site-smell found here shift and confuse the collective memories of its population.

Mark Fisher points this out in *The Weird and The Eerie*. The weird is 'that which does not belong'. The eerie is something 'partially emptied of the human'.[31] The Black Country, exemplar here of the post-industrial, is both weird and eerie: the nostalgic or belated pride is out of place and out of time, it is an uncanny relic swimming against the hyper-modern current; much of the landmarks of industrial heritage lie dormant and vacant, weeds and wildflower burst through the brickwork. It's weird because the industrial factories do not belong in this twenty-first-century landscape. It's eerie because the industrial landscapes are devoid of people, emptied of human presence once physically connected to places, regions and locales is a movement to a world where 'we ourselves are caught up in the rhythms, pulsions and patternings of non-human forces. There is no inside except as a folding of the outside'.[32,33] Part of this eerie emptiness is the previously mentioned sanitised and dulled olfactory landscape; imagine yourself in the shoes of an ex-miner, returning to the closed works that are now emptied of the sensory data that has had such a profound impact on his place-identity.

This eeriness goes further too. As with many other post-industrial areas, in the liminal post-industrial realm of the Black Country, you are surrounded by reminders of the past, but with no solid concrete left to anchor yourself to; you become a liminal identity—uncanny and in-between. Freud defines the Uncanny as a state between familiar and unfamiliar. Arguing that:

> on the one hand, it means that which is familiar and congenial, and on the other, that which is concealed and kept out of sight [...] everything is uncanny that ought to have remained hidden and secret, and yet comes to light.[34]

You can read this region's relationship with communal memory and place-identity in these terms too—one that is present and not, real and unreal, remembered and imagined. The Uncanny is not merely the unknown or a fear of the unknown. It is the ambivalence caused by the clash of known and unknown. Freud asserts: 'something has to be added to what is novel and unfamiliar to make it uncanny'[35] and positions it as 'a sub-species of heimlich'.[36] Freud argues that experiencing the uncanny is a return of the repressed, a state in which the subject finds itself confronted with something that reminds them of pre-consciousness, before the law of the father, before the super-ego. It is more than just a position of novelty and fear it is a 'class of the terrifying which leads back to something long known to us, once very familiar'.[37] The dirty self of the past invades the now cleaned-up, orientated being. It is something that one rejects and wishes to embrace—in that paradox it becomes a puzzle that needs to be solved or quarantined. For Hugh Haughton it is 'the sublime territory of unfamiliarity itself [...] a paradoxical mark of modernity. It is associated with moments when one experiences the return of the primitive in an apparently modern and secular context'.[38] In terms of place-identity and the Black Country, we can think of the uncanniness of place as both the dirty thing of the past, as well as the wholesome safe thing of the past, always on the periphery reminding us of our uncomfortable pasts. I argue that this gives rise to a liminal, marginal, uncanny or off-kilter place-identity.

Freud's Uncanny links usefully with Julia Kristeva's ideas on abjection. She defines its characteristics as:

> There looms, within abjection, one of those violent, dark revolts of being, directed against a threat that seems to emanate from an exorbitant outside or inside, ejected beyond the scope of the possible, the tolerable, the thinkable. It lies there, quite close, but it cannot be assimilated. It beseeches, worries, and fascinates desire, which, nevertheless, does not let itself be seduced.[39]

Much like the uncanny, abjection disrupts our orderly symbolic realm, reminding us of the self prior to entering subjectivity. It is the haunting of that which we deliberately cast out. Kristeva suggests that '[t]he abject confronts us [...] with our earliest attempts to release the hold of maternal entity even before ex-isting outside of her, thanks to the autonomy of language. It is a violent, clumsy breaking away.[40] We experience the abject as 'a longing to fall back into the maternal chora as well as a deep anxiety over the possibility of losing one's subjectivity'.[41] This feeling is uncanny and ambivalent because we face 'the constant risk of falling back under the sway of a power as securing as it is stifling'.[42] Abjection is an experience of disgust at something, but in that repulsion is a strange familiarity or attraction.[43] The experience is ambivalent, weird and eerie. We are faced with processing something that has been locked away, stored in the unconscious, lost in the pre-language, pre-socialised part of our psyche. Yet, at the same time, we face it in our awakened, logical, social realm of consciousness. It is the meeting place of the maternal chora and our subjectivity. Or, focusing back to the Black Country—the meeting place of identity, in the present, forged from a (imagined) past, that is always only on the periphery—a borderland.

Lacan thinks of this borderland as a state where one cannot distinguish good from bad, pleasure from displeasure. He uses the term *L'angoisse*—loosely translated as anxiety or angst, saying:

> Anxiety, as we know, is always connected with a loss – i.e. a transformation of the ego – with a two-sided relation on the point of fading away to be superseded by something else, something which the patient cannot face without vertigo. This is the realm and the nature of anxiety.[44]

In her reading of Lacan's lectures, Joan Copjec argues that Lacanian anxiety is 'the disjunction that defines displacement, which suddenly impresses itself as a gap or break in perception'.[45] As such, L'Angoisse is analogous to The Uncanny and Abjection; it is something torn away from the mundane and forces the subject into an in-between. Lacan states:

> it implies the relationship of a dimension to something different which comes to interfere with it and which entangles [...] he encounters this intimate break very close at hand, and why? Because of allowing himself to be captured en route by his own image, by the specular image. That is the trap.[46]

Conflict and ambivalence are at its core. Jacob Blevins suggests that one 'negotiates the paradoxical relationship between difference and sameness—between the Symbolic and the Imaginary—and he proposes that it is indeed "anxiety" that occupies the gap between the two.[47] What is most important in terms of this is the break in perception that causes the subject to experience loss or lack. This absence is the source of *L'Angoisse*, 'When you no longer know what to do with yourself, when you do not find anything behind which to barricade yourself [...] is what happens in subjects when the little pegs no longer go into the little holes'.[48] Freud, Kristeva and Lacan show that a significant aspect of coming into being or negotiating selfhood, is one of being incomplete, of lacking something. This incompleteness and lacking, however, has more power to it than just a gap or breakage—it becomes a quarry or cavern of unruly selfhood that is part of us and not, attractive and repulsive, familiar and unfamiliar. In short, we are liminal. We are formed from a lack or gap, and in that gap is a part of us that not only is lost forever, but is itself between states and threatening to rise up. This is, I argue, the borderland of self-hood. It is these uncanny, abject and in-between experiences that might rise up or come into fruition when one is in a liminal space, place or time. This is Mark Fisher territory again—the weird and the eerie. Paying particular attention to new and radical movements in culture, and with specific consideration to ghostly landscapes, he calls the weird 'a signal that the concepts and frameworks which we have previously employed are now obsolete'.[49] The eerie is that which acts as a 'disengagement from our current attachments'.[50] He goes on to argue that these examples of strangeness are both pleasurable and unpleasant: 'there is an enjoyment in seeing the familiar and conventional become outmoded'.[51]

Place is fundamental to selfhood and the Black Country is an example of this simultaneously weird and eerie place, I argue that it gives rise to a doubly liminal identity—one in keeping with the rebellious, the unruly, the marginalised. In the Black Country, you do not find yourself just in the border between two worlds (the past and present; the real and mythical)—one inhabits several perceptions of worlds that continuously intersect in time and place, one walks a plurality of borders between several zones.

Trigg suggests that the uncanny, and its unruly disquiet is at the core of remembering the body, and thus ourselves. Proust problematises memory in *The Prisoner*, describing it as an oblivion that springs forth randomly, presenting us with 'dead recollections'. These link with Freud's thinking—understanding the uncanny as an 'involuntary reminder' of the pre-socialised self, the return to a more feral, bodily being. Terdiman recognises this and says that 'the process of memory carries an uncanny danger',[52] and that it is both authentic and inauthentic, real and unreal, 'its representations make an absence present'.[53]

Becker talks about this in *The Denial of Death*, arguing that part of being is a conflict between the ego and the body—the megalomaniac or narcissistic tendencies of understanding culture and our centredness within it, versus the decaying organic matter that shits and fucks and vomits and sleeps and eventually dies. Becker argues that we can't understand the world without the ego, but left to its own devices we become lost. We need the animal/fleshy experiences as a way of sustaining.

With all this in mind then, we might start to see the abject or the uncanny as experiences that pull the immortality seeking ego back to body, a memory tool that stops us flying too close to the sun. In short, we need the strong foundations of place-identity, something physical to touch, smell, taste, hear and see that fixes itself to our communal memories. We need smell, the invisible sense, dare I say the uncanny or eerie sense, that summons the patchwork quilts of place-identity. In the digital age, the sensory information that harnesses and strengthens our communal memories is vital for the upkeep of place-specific wellbeing. It is a psychic leesh, preventing the pull of the cyber abyss.

Notes

1. Harold Proshansky, Abbe K. Fabien and Robert Kaminoff, 'Place Identity; Physical World Socialization of the Self', *Journal of Environmental Psychology* 3 (1983): 57–83; 59.
2. Charis E. Anton and Carmen Lawrence, 'Home Is Where the Heart Is: The effect of Place of Residence on Place Attachment and Community Participation', *Journal of Environmental Psychology* 40 (2014): 451–461; 452.
3. Darren Clarke, Conor Murphy and Irene Lorenzoni, 'Place Attachment, Disruption and Transformative Adaptation', *Journal of Environmental Psychology* 55 (2018): 81–89; 82.
4. Clare L. Tigger-Ross and David L. Uzzell, 'Place and Identity Process', *Journal of Environmental Psychology* 16 (1996): 205–220; 206.
5. Tigger-Ross and Uzzell, 207.
6. Richard H. Rijnks and Dirk Strijker, 'Spatial Effects on the Image and Identity of a Rural Area', *Journal of Environmental Psychology* 36 (2013): 103–111; 103–104.
7. Rijnks and Strijker, 107.
8. Tigger-Ross and Uzzell, 207.
9. Tigger-Ross and Uzzell, 208.
10. Clarke, Murphy, Lorenzoni, 82.
11. Tigger-Ross and Uzzell, 207–208.
12. Ed McMahon, *Where Am I? The Power of Uniqueness*, Jacksonville TEDTalk, https://www.youtube.com/watch?v=qB5tH4rt-x8 published 06/01/15, [Accessed 01/08/17], Unpaginated.

13. McMahon, ibid.
14. James Whale was the director of 1930s Universal Classic Horrors *Franken-stein* (1931), *Bride of Frankenstein* (1935) and *The Invisible Man* (1933): there's a memorial in the car park of Castlegate enterprise zone.
15. Ed McMahon, ibid.
16. Anton and Lawrence, 453.
17. Clarke, Murphy and Lorenzoni, 83.
18. The Black Country Studies Centre is a research centre founded by the University of Wolverhampton and the Black Country Living Museum. See http://blackcountrystudiescentre.co.uk.
19. Ned Williams, *Dudley & Netherton Remembered* (Stroud: The History Press, 2010), 109.
20. Williams, *Dudley & Netherton Remembered*, 109.
21. Ned Williams, *Netherton: People and Places* (Stroud: The History Press, 2008), 5.
22. Ned Williams, *Netherton: People and Places*, 7–8.
23. Joana J. Bryson, 'Simulation and the Evolution of Thought', in *Memory in the Twenty-First Century*, edited by Sebastian Groes (New York: Palgrave Macmillan, 2016), 205–208.
24. Sean O'Brien, 'As Deep As England: The Newcastle/Bloodaxe Poetry Lectures 2011', *Poetry Review* 102, no. 1 (Spring 2012): 54–69.
25. O'Brien, 54.
26. O'Brien, 55.
27. O'Brien, 55.
28. O'Brien, 58.
29. Marc Augé', *Non-places: Introduction to an Anthropology of Supermodernity*, trans John Howe (London: Verso, 1995), 120.
30. Fredric Jameson, *Postmodernism: Or, the Cultural Logic of Late Capitalism* (Durham: Duke University Press, 1991), 15.
31. Mark Fisher, *The Weird and the Eerie* (London: Repeater Book, 2016), 10–11.
32. Fisher, 9.
33. Fisher, 9.
34. Sigmund Freud, *The Uncanny*, trans. David McLintock (London: Penguin, 2003), 4.
35. Freud, 2.
36. Freud, 4.
37. Freud, 1.

38. Hugh Haughton, *Introduction* to *The Uncanny*, trans. David McLintock (London: Penguin, 2003), xlix.
39. Julia Kristeva, *Powers of Horror: An Essay on Abjection*, trans. Leon S. Roudiez (Columbia: Columbia University Press, 1982), 1.
40. Kristeva, 14.
41. McAfee, 47.
42. Kristeva, 14.
43. Like Freud, Kristeva provides examples of the abject: toxic waste; corpses, egg yolk, vomit, bodily fluids, the film that settles on milk or custard.
44. Jacques Lacan and Wladimir Granoff, 'Fetishism: The Symbolic, the Imaginary and the Real', in *Paru dans Perversions: Psychodynamics and Therapy* (New York: Random-House Inc, 1956), 265–276; 270.
45. Joan Copjec, 'May '68 The Emotional Month', in *Lacan: The Silent Partners*, edited by Slavoj Zizek (London: Verso 2006), 90–115; 96.
46. Jacques Lacan, *The Seminar of Jacques Lacan: Book X Anxiety 1962–1963*, trans. Cormac Gallagher, http://www.lacaninireland.com/web/wp-con tent/uploads/2010/06/Seminar-X-Revised-by-Mary-Cherou-Lagreze.pdf [Accessed 06/03/16], 8.
47. Jacob Blevins, 'Influence, Anxiety, and the Symbolic: A Lacanian Rereading of Bloom', *Intertexts* 9, no. 2 (Fall 2005): 123–138; 127.
48. Lacan, *Seminar X*, 9–11.
49. Fisher, 14.
50. Fisher, 14.
51. Fisher, 13.
52. Richard Terdiman, *Present Past: Modernity and the Memory Crisis* (London: Cornell University Press, 1993), 108.
53. Terdiman, 108.

Works Cited

Anton, Charis E. and Carmen Lawrence. 'Home Is Where the Heart Is: The Effect of Place of Residence on Place Attachment and Community Participation', *Journal of Environmental Psychology* 40 (2014): 451–461.
Augé, Marc. *Non-places: Introduction to an Anthropology of Supermodernity*, trans John Howe (London: Verso, 1995).

Blevins, Jacob. 'Influence, Anxiety, and the Symbolic: A Lacanian Rereading of Bloom', *Intertexts* 9, no. 2 (Fall 2005): 123–138.

Bryson, Joana, 'Simulation and the Evolution of Thought', in *Memory in the Twenty-First Century*, edited by Sebastian Groes (New York: Palgrave Macmillan, 2016).

Clarke, Darren, Conor Murphy and Irene Lorenzoni. 'Place Attachment, Disruption and Transformative Adaptation', *Journal of Environmental Psychology* 55 (2018): 81–89.

Copjec, Joan. 'May '68 The Emotional Month', in *Lacan: The Silent Partners*, edited by Slavoj Zizek (London: Verso, 2006), 90–115.

Fisher, Mark. *The Weird and the Eerie* (London: Repeater Book, 2016).

Freud, Sigmund. *The Uncanny*, trans. David McLintock (London: Penguin, 2003).

Haughton, Hugh. *Introduction* to *The Uncanny*, trans. David McLintock (London: Penguin, 2003).

Jameson, Fredric. *Postmodernism: Or, the Cultural Logic of Late Capitalism* (Durham: Duke University Press, 1991).

Kristeva, Julia. *Powers of Horror: An Essay on Abjection*, trans. Leon S. Roudiez (Columbia: Columbia University Press, 1982).

Lacan, Jacques. *The Seminar of Jacques Lacan: Book X Anxiety 1962–1963*, trans. Cormac Gallagher. http://www.lacaninireland.com/web/wp-content/uploads/2010/06/Seminar-X-Revised-by-Mary-Cherou-Lagreze.pdf [Accessed 06/03/19].

Lacan, Jacques and Wladimir Granoff. 'Fetishism: The Symbolic, the Imaginary and the Real', in *Paru dans Perversions: Psychodynamics and Therapy* (New-York: Random House, 1956), 65–276.

McMahon, Ed. *Where Am I? The Power of Uniqueness*, Jacksonville TEDTalk. https://www.youtube.com/watch?v=qB5tH4rt-x8 published 06/01/2015 [Accessed 01/08/2017].

O'Brien, Sean. 'As Deep As England: The Newcastle/Bloodaxe Poetry Lectures 2011', *Poetry Review* 102, no. 1 (Spring 2012): 54–69.

Proshansky, Harold, Abbe K. Fabien and Robert Kaminoff. 'Place Identity: Physical World Socialization of the Self', *Journal of Environmental Psychology* 3 (1983): 57–83.

Rijnks, Richard and Dirk Strijker. 'Spatial Effects on the Image and Identity of a Rural Area', *Journal of Environmental Psychology* 36 (2013): 103–111.

Tigger-Ross, Claire and David Uzzell. 'Place and Identity Process', *Journal of Environmental Psychology* 16 (1996): 205–220.

Terdiman, Richard. *Present Past: Modernity and the Memory Crisis* (Ithaca and New York: Cornell University Press, 1993).

Williams, Ned. *Dudley & Netherton Remembered* (Stroud: The History Press, 2010).

Williams, Ned. *Netherton: People and Places* (Stroud: The History Press, 2008).

14

We Try to Keep Sunday Best, Though Mom Hates Sundays

Natalie Burdett

After church, we'd drink Irn Bru,
wipe beefy crisp-crumbs from faces with the backs of hands
as mom and dad pulled out the twin tub,
pushed it to the sink to fill,
its whir spreading chlorine's shock
through heavy whites,
bleach mist making windows opaque.

Our boredom simmered
with the powder's garden-fresh green flecks.
Their faces reddened
hauling dripping towels from washer to spinner
like drowned otters on the boiler stick –
bone-pale, cracked but strengthened by hot-cold dry-wet.

N. Burdett (✉)
Manchester Metropolitan University, Manchester, UK

Last, the dark load's incense and grit
swirled the space-pattern drum
with soft rinse water – slippy, blue –
gathered a tang of rubber
splurging through the curved grey pipe,
then a final tipping up.
A cabbage pan rattling, too, now

mixing iron with clean steam
fat spitting in the pudding tray – hot, dangerous,
roast potatoes – salt crisp,
turkey roast shrinking from its paper wrap – meat fat,
the brittle smell of the oven's glass door,
the dog under mom's feet
and us not helping
and homework not even started yet.

15

An Idea Once Crystalised

Emma Purshouse

Maybe it was a weird thing to do
to send a paper bag full of suck
in the post, not so much as a note,

their smell permeating the jiffy bag
waiting to waft out into your room,
that heady mix of the medicinal

and the factory filling your air with
the sort of smell you might put on a wound
or a scratch where the swarf has bit.

The sort of smell that might,
one cold night, remind you of
home, of me, of the Black Country.

E. Purshouse (✉)
Wolverhampton, UK

S. Groes et al. (eds.), *Smell, Memory, and Literature in the Black Country*,
https://doi.org/10.1007/978-3-030-57212-9_15

16

Olfactory Pathways to Black Country Futures

Stuart Connor

Thinking Future

This chapter provides accounts of embodied practices in conditions that, although inherited, have been re-cast to comport sensorial spaces that enable explorations of what it can mean to be and dwell within the Black Country. Particular attention is drawn to the questions of if and how odours, and the rest of our senses for that matter, play a role not just in re-remembering our past but in helping to summon our futures.

The visceral power of odour-evoked memories is well documented in the arts and sciences.[1] Odour-evoked memory, both the ability to recognise and remember whether one has smelled an odour before and when an odour conjures a meaningful memory or associations is a remarkable feature of our everyday experience. But what role do smells have for anticipating and shaping futures? When discussing the nature of the future, de Jouvenel draws attention to a distinction in Latin between

S. Connor (✉)
University of Wolverhampton, Wolverhampton, UK

© The Author(s), under exclusive license to Springer
Nature Switzerland AG 2021
S. Groes et al. (eds.), *Smell, Memory, and Literature in the Black Country*,
https://doi.org/10.1007/978-3-030-57212-9_16

143

Facta, past events that are 'done' and *futura*, events that have yet to come about.[2] An extension of this distinction is that *facta* are phenomena that have been experienced, whereas *futura* cannot be experienced as they are yet to come. The yet to come nature of *futura* would appear to make redundant a project that seeks to explore olfactory pathways to futures, for if the future has not happened yet, how can it be experienced through the senses. However, this chapter departs from a view of time as a container that includes discrete now, past and future moments, as evident in the distinction between *facta* and *futura*.

There is a diverse, distinct and significant tradition of writing[3] that has sought to question a metaphysics of presence.[4] In contrast to a vulgar conception of time, where the present is viewed as a distinct event within a timeline along which you move, time is experienced as what Henri Bergson calls *durée*.[5] This sense of duration is intimate yet inscrutable and resists attempts at capture and expression.[6] A mode of experience, three ecstases of past, present and future, are understood as three dimensions of our experience that extend in time in a distinctive but mutually constitutive and complementary way.[7] Each of these ecstases is not separate intentional acts, but consanguineous elements, often in the background but essential to each intent.[8] It is not the past that determines the present, but the future that leads by engaging the other two ecstases of past and present.[9] Steered and motivated by futures, time flows from anticipated futures, back to the past and through to a present. An agent chooses themselves in their projects, which discloses the significance of the choices made from the array of possibilities afforded by the shared worlds into which you may have been thrown and summons the significance of the present situation.[10]

Within the everyday, senses reflect and realise this intuitive flow of time and experience. Redolent of the analogy of melodies, senses are vital to connecting the alleged discrete moments of a vulgar conception of time.[11] Smells offer an olfactory melody that simultaneously anticipates future states, evokes a recalling of a summoned past and attends to, immerses, but also transcends a rich but transient present. Senses offer a vivid articulation of the concatenation of retention, attention and protention[12] that constitutes everyday futures—our dwelling with the world.[13]

An initial clue and instance of this sense of the temporal and the role of smell in the shaping of our futures can be found in the most every day of experiences. A particular odour, the deep fried salt and vinegary smell of a local chippy, or the rich mix of turmeric, garlic and cumin from a Vaisakhi Festival, not only evokes memories or associations, but also cues a visceral response, most likely an increased salivation, at the anticipation of the sights, tastes, textures and feelings to come.

A smell can alert us to a possibility that we may have not been previously alert to. Think of how the smell of a roast dinner from a neighbour's house can wrench us from our routine, remind us that it has been a while since such a meal has been shared and for such a meal to become, for the moment at least, prioritised in our plans. Or conversely, how the smell may repel us and steel our resolve and commitment to veganism. In this regard, a sensed future's potency to shape and affect our experience of the world lies in the possibilities that are revealed and how the anticipation of something that is not currently present, can change not just our awareness of things but the significance of things.

Whether it is the oft cited Proustian rush of a *petites madeleine*,[14] the sensory epiphany of the critic Anton Ego in the film Ratatouille[15] or the smell of the chippy noted above, the senses offer tangible insights into structural facets of our experience of time. To explore such olfactory pathways to Black Country futures further, this chapter shares three vignettes, *Fighting Gravity*, *Weightless Mass* and *Life's Allotment*. Created using a combination of participant observation and ready-made documents, the purpose of these vignettes is to draw attention to the potentially radical aspects of sites, practices and phenomena that are frequently dismissed as marginal and peripheral to understandings of the Black Country and the shaping of futures.

These vignettes foreground the value of the everyday to shaping futures, the role of futures in the everyday and the vital role of the senses and corporeality in these routine futures. The vignettes detail sites and practices where thinking, acting and feeling are interrelated and irreducible strands that constitute a dynamic movement to different ways of being. By examining the emergent entanglement of particular routines, the chapter illustrates the way in which everyday practices open out and close down the capacities and affective atmospheres for different ways of being and prefigure different forms of being in the future.

It is argued that, although not in the form of vision statements or executable programmes and plans,[16] that each of the routines detailed in these vignettes contains an 'anticipatory' dimension.[17] Within the concept of *durée* where time is heterogeneous and dynamic, if anything can be thought of as enduring, like the Ship of Theseus or Trigger's well-maintained broom,[18] it is through divergence and transformation.[19] A negotiation of the complexities of time and becoming,[20] discourses, images, and practices not only disrupt received and predominant ways of being but also explore and pre-figure what it is to be.[21] One of the reasons for this is that the world is not fixed or finished. A source of anxiety, our contingency is also the source of our greatest hope and dignity as beings because recurring conjunctures afford new possibilities and pathways. The way we understand ourselves is always open to question, an issue yet to be resolved. If I am to discover the world in my own way, a great deal of effort needs to go into clearing away concealments and obscurities and gathering and summoning conditions, experiences and dispositions.[22] This is not a search that can be undertaken solely through a detached, rational, analytic or reflective exercise, but a revealing and a dwelling, expressed and enacted by and through the senses. It is not about 'looking' at the truth, but awakening our experience of it.[23]

Fighting Gravity

With origins in Walsall, but franchised in Dudley, Wolverhampton and West Bromwich, these are industrial premises, occupied and repurposed for a new set of demands. Cold in winter and an oven in summer. On a busy night cars are strewn outside in every available space. As you zig-zag to the door, taking care not to step in the puddled potholes, the bass of the soundtrack, punctured by the shrill clanking of iron bars, gets louder and deeper. The door opens and you are enveloped by the light, sound and smells of 'The Foundry'. Following a brief flurry of nods, you prepare to train and the routine begins.

A strange brew of sinus and throat bothering citrus and bleach effusing cleaning products hangs in the air and is in competition with the raw sweat that is the by-product of training. Sensory landmarks populate this unique 'scentscape'. Brewed coffee blends with the saccharine sweetness of low-calorie protein mixes at the counter. Whiffs of designer fragrancies follow fellow gym users as they move from station to station. A dry cloak of chalk and the piquant and tingling traces of camphor and menthol that make up the muscle rubs are not uncommon on the lifting platforms. Occasionally, like an uninvited guest, clouds of cigarette smoke impose themselves from outside. Periodically humid clouds of shower gel and talcum powder occupy the changing rooms and it would be amiss not to note, but advisable not to dwell, on the legacy of the protein rich diets that gather menacingly in the toilets. None of these can be described as particularly pleasant odours, but they are the products and markers of this place.

One place but many programmes, each one with its own means and ends.[24] Powerlifting, bodybuilding, classic or open, strength and conditioning, cross fit, weightlifting, functional fitness, cardio or strength. It might be about getting bigger and leaner, winning trophies, getting ready for the beach or your socials. You may just be seeking to recapture a lost youth or arrest an inevitable decay of the body, but they all involve a journey of many small steps. Persistent, progressive efforts are common and essential to all such sustained projects. There are transgressors, the show boats, the talkers, the 'instas', the dawdlers and the hoggers, but for those who last, to endure, it can't just be about appearances.[25]

The routines of the gym, the same gym, the same time, and what appear to be the same programmes, the same soundtracks, the same barbells, the same machines, the same sets, the same reps and the same movements can appear dull and boring. To the uninitiated, the patterns and rhythm are nothing more than poignant echoes of the machines of an industrial age that once occupied these spaces. Then people operated machines. Now, people are operating as machines.[26] And yet, it is in these mechanical, incremental and quantifiable aspects of training that many can and do find a meaning, an extended sense of being. The gym can offer users a chance to pursue clear and measurable goals with outcomes that can be traced directly back to oneself.[27] However, this does not tell the full story.

Results do matter, but the anticipated results are slow to emerge and even when reached, tend to be denigrated and extended. No, for many, what keeps you in the gym, and coming back for each, day, each week, each month, again and again and again, is how it makes you feel, how it brings you back to your senses.[28] What keeps you going is the not the prospect of the journey, but the experience of each step. You need to imagine Sisyphus happy.[29] Lifting demands that you attend to what you are doing right now and attending and un-concealing aspects of experience all too readily overshadowed. The mirrors offer a guide to the movement, but it is the mind's eye and your senses, including the sixth sense of kinaesthesia, that best ensures the necessary mind muscle connection that visualises, feels and experiences the sliding and contraction of the myosin and actin filaments. It is now that all your senses play a part in gaining a greater sense of who you are.

On particularly demanding sets, the ammonia from the smelling salts, invades and provokes a reflex. Your pattern of breathing is altered. You are alerted and attendant to what follows. As the set progresses, strains are felt in different places as the weak links in your chain are outed. A lip is bitten and sweat bleads into the corner of your mouth, a metallic hue of iron and salt can be tasted. A failing grip and the engorged feelings of the infamous pump impede your progress. Your breathing seeks to dowse the burning of lactic acidosis. Mental contracts are signed to help get you to the end of the set. Shaky but determined, your senses do not only provide a guide to whether the correct path is being followed, but also offers a sensory destination. Your body is no longer defined by how it looks or what it can do. For the moment at least your body is no longer a resource to be deployed by others or yourself towards a particular goal, but something to be experienced. Your thoughts, feelings and actions coalesce into a visceral way of being, where you are able to dwell in all that your body is. The weight of your being gives rise to a satisfying and satiating feeling.

The attention and value that such an account places on attending to the present, the body and the senses may appear to be at odds with a discussion of everyday futures, but here is the paradox. The now and the future are not in contradiction. These are concrete actions that realise and reflect anticipations that prefigure and summon real possibilities for the future—not just a different version of you in the future, but an extended sense of what it is to be. Attending to now and being alert through and to my senses is vital to the future that I am shaping. To be human is to be beyond ourselves. It is this way that the gym offers the promise of a transformative practice. Ceaselessly becoming, a consciousness of the present becomes possible within a horizon of possible futures.

Weightless Mass

Built it the 1970s, the distinctive hexagonal shape of St Joseph's R.C. Church Darlaston, echoes the form of the steel nuts that remain a significant part of the local industry. A black tiled roof, topped with a tall slender fibreglass spire, crowns a steel framed and red bricked construction. Inside, exposed tubular steel stanchions and a frame of girders are completed with brickwork. As you enter the church, you are faced with a large crucifix set behind and above the high altar, which in turn is set upon a small, staggered rise of marble steps.

Led by the Thurifer and a cross bearer, a solemn procession of the priest and altar servers leaves the sacristy. As the procession passes through the congregation, the thurible is swung back and forth. At the end of the brass chains the weight of the censure forms a transient arc. Small clouds of incense punctuate the end of each swing and slowly drift across the congregation. As the procession reaches its destination, the priest takes the thurible and with the chain shortened, continues to cast its cloud, addressing and circling the altar. The sparse and wispy traces of scent issued with each swing now begin, ever so briefly to gather and rise and above the altar, before dissipating again into the most immaterial of presences.

References and prescriptions for the use of incense have ancient theological origins. In Exodus,[30]

34The Lord said to Moses, "Take sweet spices, stacte, and onycha, and galbanum, sweet spices with pure frankincense (of each shall there be an equal part), 35and make an incense blended as by the perfumer, seasoned with salt, pure and holy. 36You shall beat some of it very small, and put part of it before the testimony in the tent of meeting where I shall meet with you. It shall be most holy for you. 37And the incense that you shall make according to its composition, you shall not make for yourselves. It shall be for you holy to the Lord.

The use of incense during Mass is intended to communicate to, through and beyond our senses that we have entered into the sacred. The Catholic Church incorporates the use of incense during the Mass to symbolise the smoke of purification and sanctification. The use of incense in this way is referenced in the scripture by St. John in the Apocalypse as he describes his vision of the heavenly worship, where an Angel holds a golden censer near the altar, upon which stands the lamb. Incense is also understood to represent the prayers of the faithful rising to heaven, 'Let my prayer be counted as incense before you, and the lifting up of my hands as the evening sacrifice!'[31]

Different formulations of incense are available; there is the potential for each parish to have its own distinct aroma, though they are frequently made up with aromatics such as frankincense and myrrh. A complex and undulating aroma, the spicy, liquorice and warm yet bitter notes of myrrh is combined with the complex, pungent, piny and woody warmth of Frankincense. Sweet, sensual and clean, the scent is ineluctable. With an etymology of *eluctari*, to struggle out of, the unavoidable and inevitable, the use of incense within the Mass communicates to our olfactory receptors that we are in a sacred place. A scent distinct from the world one has just left; this is not an aroma or experience to be identified with the hum drum of daily life.

The daylight is filtered by the coloured glass of the windows and weaves with the spots of candlelight scattered around the church. Each of the wooden and stone figures is individually lit and brings a warm tone to their surfaces. The words, the music, the rhythm, and a choral cordiality echo through the space and over time. But it is the silences, pierced by a bell, that resonate. A silence, an intentional silence, can jar. What do you attend to? A space is cleared. An absence un-conceals a presence—a presence that was always there. Occupying the silence and blurring the boundaries between yourself and space is the now deeply diffused scent of the incense.

You can attend Mass for weeks, months and years and just take your place within the congregation as the service unfolds. Occasionally you can witness the slightly awkward movements and delays of people unfamiliar with the passage of the service, but more often than not, this is a group well-rehearsed and aligned with the order of the day. On occasions though, for some more than others, for others, maybe never, the service can affect in unexpected ways.[32] Difficult to describe and possibly even more difficult to understand, you can just open up, a weight lifts and a timorous shudder can be felt. Sometimes accompanied by a smile, sometimes you just sit back and cry. Not from within or without, a simultaneous reception and release are felt.

Distinct affective atmospheres of the sacred or the divine are evoked and enacted through objects, images, texts, architecture and most notably the senses.[33] There is a somatic and kinaesthetic dimension to religious practice.[34] Belief becomes enfolded into an experience of the sensory world.[35] What is taken to be the most of immaterial of experiences, the spiritual, can be heightened, facilitated and expressed through the performance of the service where the transcendental is made sense-able'.[36] Smell, sound, rhythms and touch combine and intersect to summon a mood and affective atmosphere that anticipates and realises, not just a different way of being, but an extended sense of what it means to be. Openness to a spiritual way of being can be facilitated and manifest in the most material and effusive corporeal sensations, an 'inner warmth', 'goose pimples' and 'tears'. Prior beliefs can and do play an important role in cultivating a faithful sensibility and disposition, but it is the body and mind, as one, that is opened up to perceive and feel new sensorial and performative possibilities and manifestations of 'absent presences' ascribed to nonhuman agents and higher powers. The ultimate origin of such affects may be in question, a question of belief, but the desire and recognition of experiences that seek to extend beyond our material projects and the role of senses in these experiences is very real.

In a profane and transient world, where everything can be made available and we become available to them, one can understand a search for a sense of the sacred, the enduring and the presence of that which is in reach, but unavailable. A Mass and its engagement with all the senses embody a contradiction. The most immediate, tangible and empirical experience of taste, sound, touch, sight and smell, can also evoke the most remote, intangible and immaterial states and ways of being, an understanding and experience that we can be both body and spirit.

Life's Allotment

A five-minute walk from Darlaston town centre, parallel to the cutting and before the swimming baths is a crescent length of railing and a metal gate. In contrast to the long road that sweeps around the site, beyond the boundary and small car park, lies a quilted collection of plots of land and sheds, tenuously tethered by the slimmest network of paths. On any given day a loose collection of individuals can be found tending to their allotment.

The sun is still low and the air is crisp. The matting is rolled back. Attention to this part of the plot is long overdue. It is a good fork, it comes recommended, but the heavy clay and successive steps make the digging particularly hard work. An initial enthusiasm to get the job done is quickly tempered by the effort involved. Sweat gathers. Callouses begin to bubble and form, a shoulder aches from the awkward dull jabs, your back and hamstrings strain and your body arcs into an uncommon figure. Your body makes itself known. Swapping hands, switching body positions and new angles of attack all seek to mitigate the discomforts of the task. Then a semblance of a rhythm begins to develop.

A light breeze carries the smells of neighbouring plots and the surrounding streets and houses. The sun tends to your cheeks, neck and hands. The sweet distinctive aromas of the tomatoes, rocket and strawberries are the legacy of your work to date and a foreshadowing of future tastes. Your mind wanders from the pondering of plans for this patch, to weighing up the options for the distribution and consumption of the abundance to come.[37] A sweet bubble gum candy imbued tang from a passer-by's vaping brings you back to the plot. A distinct plume from a passing car exhaust suggests that the engine is burning oil. The acrid smell of wet wood being burned in a nearby stove introduces itself and grates—that is not allowed.

Down at your feet, the dark matter, with attention, reveals the forms that sustain and threaten your projects. Worms are in evidence. Flies inspect the disturbed earth. Beetles traverse the fresh burrows. You stoop to clear the latest collections of stones, 'half enders' and assorted detritus of the past thirty years—Lego bricks, hot wheels cars, broken bottle bottoms, screws, nails and shreds of plastic. The soil does not look, feel or smell promising. More dank decay than rich resource, but you have to work with what you have got. There is no other place to start than here.

A huge appeal of the allotment is the physicality of the place.[38] This can be experienced and expressed by the labour that is extended in the bodily working that the plot requires.[39] The bone-tired feeling at the end of the evening, a self-imposed duress rather than distress is satisfying. The matter of the soil, plants, compost, tools, etc. also matter.[40] Learning to read the qualities of these materials is a vital part of any successful project, but also requires and engages a range of senses and practices. Then of course there is the experience of exposing yourself to all of the elements that the plot affords—the changing weather, sounds, light and smells. A favourite is the crisp, still, clean freshness that follows a summer shower, but even the plunge and enveloping of a boot in a saturated soil has its satisfactions—particularly when followed by drying off in the shed, with a sweet cup of tea and biscuits.

Your mind wanders again; your nails are filthy. You smile. The room note of pipe smoke weaves its ways across—its origin, possibly a pensioner or a hipster, remains anonymous. You reminisce about your Aunt and Uncle who used to bring their surplus leeks and potatoes to the house when you were a kid. The distinct draught of earthy freshness embarrassed the other plastic wrapped food stuffs in your house and served as a prompt to your own interest in growing. The rain eases. You survey your sensorial realm. Proximate, but far removed from the daily demands and structured schedules of the world, this is a place where it is not only advisable, but necessary to attend and align to the rhythms of the day, the season and the year. It is time to resume. That patch is not going to weed itself. Your joints have settled into place and require some care and coaxing to continue. It will take a little time to ease past the inertia of this break, but a careful tending is all that is required.

The plot is a site where touch, sight, sound, taste and smells are vital to the means, ends and meaning of a project.[41] Yes, the allotment can produce food and increasingly acts as an important resource for the necessities of life and a sense of belonging, but it also offers a rare opportunity in an urban conurbation, to connect with and blur the distinctions between your body and nature.[42] The senses are responses to, cues for and the expression of experiences that flow and jar and require continual embodied negotiations and cognitive adjustments. An irreducible confluence of thoughts, feelings, senses and actions, blurs mind and body, body and world, process and product. The allotment is not only a retreat from the routines of daily life, but also represents an advance into a way of being that rethinks your relationship with the world. This is not a place where demands can be made and controlled, but one that requires an ongoing tending and attention to its nature.

Definite Possibilities

The world into which we are thrown offers a repository of affordances for living. The dispositions we have for the world both emerge from and influence the way the world itself is set up to unfold. The shared worlds of the Black Country may well provide the conditions, within which new pathways and futures are shaped, but the forms of poetic praxis that emerge from the alleged routine and everyday practices, prefigure different ways of being and unconceal latent potentialities for being. Within the alleged repetitive and routine practices of everyday life, senses are vital to not only our experiences of time but revealing how we can dwell and act towards the future.

The routines in these vignettes are characterised by the desire to be or extend and enhance a feeling of being. These are practices that create forms of affectedness and a disclosive embrace with the world.[43] More than thought and action, it is a tacit, felt and extended sense of being in the world. This is not oblivion, or a sense that your being has been dissolved, but an embodied, extended and enriched way of being. This sense of being, this affectedness does not arise from within or imposed from without, but is an unconcealing and summoning of latent relations and experiences.[44] Thinking, feeling and acting constitute the irreducible elements of being. The performative aspects of practice make use of and attune the sensory capacities of the body and open up discernment capable of registering presences that resonate outside the enframements of the everyday.[45] A belief in the presence and power of something other than the given, immediate and self-evident world around us may be a prerequisite and vital to the experiencing of such experiences, but these are forms of poetic praxis where meaning and value is not derived from the ability to act in the world but a sense of being and a disposition towards being.[46]

Is this account authentically Black Country? No, if authentic is deemed as adhering to some pre-existing template or measure as to what is and is not Black Country. However, authentic can also be construed as attempts to understand being in terms of distinctive and definitive possibilities; a projection of plural pasts into labyrinthine future pathways. If understood as possibilities that are afforded through particular engagements with the resources of a specific time and place, then yes, this is authentically Black Country. The world into which we are thrown offers a repository of affordances for living. What we value, what we pursue, the clips we watch and share, the shows and music we stream, the kind of things we talk about, the food we eat, the ways we dress, the holidays we plan, our response to current events—all this is shaped by others. A network of activities and entities are aligned with one another so as to foster some dispositions and practices on our part and discourage others.

As we learn to use things that surround us in our shared world, we are subtly introduced into habits and practices and dispositions that we share with others. If the gym, church or allotment hadn't already been available, other projects may well have been pursued, but this is a simple reminder of how much of what matters requires a negotiation with what already exists and that our basic possibilities for being are dictated to us by the shared world we inhabit and constitute with others. The Black Country, both in terms of the legacy of previous generations and the activities of those within and without the area, offers a particular configuration of resources for existing in the world. The meaning of nearly everything we encounter or everything we do then is informed to a considerable degree by the fact that we always inhabit a shared world with others. This is not to say that what is described is unique to the Black Country, far from it. Rather it is just to highlight the distinct configuration of resources and trajectories that are made available, anticipated and enacted within a particular time and place.

Rather than a totalising force, the shared worlds of the Black Country provide the resources and basis upon which new pathways and futures can be shaped. These are explorations and accounts of doing, being and becoming.[47] Everyday tasks may well be inherited and explicitly concerned with reflective or programmatic instrumental projects, but they also contain the potential to offer an alternative and intuitive way of being, where no priority is granted to thinking, acting or feeling. Akin to an emergent choreography, connections between the three ecstases past, present and future and the synthesis of senses, thoughts and actions collapse vulgar distinctions and make evident the non-linearity of time. The past, is no longer a discretely bounded earlier time, but revealed with future temporalities in 'new' ways. Futures are not completely distinct from the past, but still offer a site where existing struggles, tensions and repressions can be overcome.[48] In these practices, the senses play a vital role in guiding physical activity and opening up experiences and ways of being that although not known in advance, are anticipated.

Each of these vignettes draws together bodily practices that summon definite and particular possibilities. These are concrete practices, where concrete is taken to mean tangible and specific, but also alludes to the Latin *concrescere* and refers to the coalescence of these practices. The possibilities being disclosed in these vignettes are not immaterial or free-floating possibilities, but definite possibilities that are afforded by being within and living through these times and places. This is in contrast to an inauthentic way of being where the world's existing systems determine what is valued or in contrast an imagined existence free from the gravity of our material existence. Exploring ways of being and ways to be may be universal, but the particular set of resources, dispositions and contingencies that are drawn upon and produced through these practices articulate a distinct form of Black Country, when this form of Black Country is understood as an emergent and contested phenomena.

This account can be read, but is not intended, as advocating a form of quietism or the continued by-product of the process of individualisation.[49] Admittedly, the practices described here are not to be construed as proto-political struggles in the sense that they are seeking to articulate, subscribe to or execute a political programme or blueprint. Neither are these practices concerned with ensuring the subsistence of individuals, families or community and as such, survival or coping strategies. However, it is considered to be myopic to only see these processes as little more than a mere accommodation to or 'dubious polishing of what exists'.[50]

It is argued that these routines have the potential to be understood as radical practices. The radicalness of these practices can be found in the substitution of an enframing position with efforts to unconceal and summon the conditions under which being can be explored and experienced.[51] If understood with reference to the late Latin *radicalis*, itself from Latin *radic-*, *radix*, meaning 'root', then the efforts to grasp the roots of our being means that these practices can be seen as radical. Each of these vignettes reflects embodied, extended, entangled and enacted responses to what participants find wanting in the world. What is evident is the role of senses in the summoning and sustaining of spaces that can reveal concealed capacities and affective atmospheres for being. Beyond the stated aims and method of a particular project, aspects of what it is to be a human being are opened up and experienced through the senses. These embodied critiques do not arise from a distanced reflection and analysis of a given situation, but reflect an immersive, intuitive and visceral negotiation and emergence of practices and ways of being. These realms may be entered into for the most instrumental of reasons, but what keeps you coming are the opportunities to disclose and experience different ways of being and new opportunities to be.

Notes

1. Marcel Proust, *In Search of Lost Time: The Way by Swann's Vol. 1*, trans. Lydia Davis (London: Penguin Classics, 2003); Trygg Engen, *The Perception of Odors* (New York: Academic Press, 1982); Rachel S. Herz,

'The Role of Odor-Evoked Memory on Psychological and Physiological Health', *Brain Science* 6, no. 3 (2016): 22. https://doi.org/10.3390/brains ci6030022; Willander Johann and Maria Larsson, 'Olfaction and Emotion: The Case of Autobiographical Memory', *Memory Cognition* 35, no. 7 (2007): 1659–1663. https://doi.org/10.3758/BF03193499.

2. Bertrand de Jouvenel, *The Art of Conjecture*, trans N. Lary (New Brunswick: Transaction Publishers, 2012), 3–6.

3. Barbara Adam, *Time* (Cambridge and Malden, MA: Polity, 2004); Henri Bergson, *Key Writings*, ed. Keith Ansell Pearson and John O'Maoilearca (London: Bloomsbury, 2014); Gilles Deleuze and Felix Guatarri, *Thousand Plateaus*, trans. Brian Massumi (Minneapolis, MN: University of Minnesota Press, 1987); Norbert Elias, *What Is Sociology?*, trans. Stephen Mennell and Grace Morrisey (New York: Columbia University Press, 1984); Elizabeth Grosz, *Time Travels: Feminism, Nature, Power* (Durham and London: Duke University Press, 2005); Georg Wilhelm Friedrich Hegel, *Phenomenology of Spirit* (Oxford: Oxford University Press, 1978); Heraclitus, *Fragments*, trans. Brooks Haxton (London: Penguin Classics, 500 BCE/2003); St Augustine, *Confessions*, trans. Henry Chadwick (Oxford: Oxford University Press, 2008).

4. Jaques Derrida, *Speech and Phenomena: and Other Essays on Husserl's Theory of Signs*, trans. David B. Allison (Evanston: Northwestern University, 1967/1973).

5. Bergson, *Key Writings*, 87.

6. Bergson, *Key Writings*, 93.

7. Martin Heidegger, *Being and Time*, trans. Joan Stambaugh (Albany, NY: State University of New York Press, 1953/2010).

8. John Richardson, *Heidegger* (London: Routledge, 2012).

9. Heidegger, *Being and Time*, 326.

10. Heidegger, *Being and Time*, 326.

11. Edmund Husserl, *On the Phenomenology of the Consciousness of Internal Time (1983–1917)*, trans. John Barnett Brough (Dordrecht: Kluwer Academic Publishers, 1991).

12. Edmund Husserl, *On the Phenomenology of the Consciousness of Internal Time (1983–1917)*, trans. John Barnett Brough (Dordrecht: Kluwer Academic Publishers, 1991).

13. Martin Heidegger, *Poetry, Language, Thought*, trans. Albert Hofstadter (New York, NY: Harper Perennial Modern Thought, 1971/2013).

14. Marcel Proust, *In Search of Lost Time: The Way by Swann's Vol. 1*, trans. Lydia Davis (London: Penguin Classics, 2003).

15. Marcus Bussey, 'Intimate Futures: Bringing the Body into Futures Work', *European Journal of Futures Research* 53, no. 2 (2014). https://doi.org/10.1007/s40309-014-0053-6.
16. Marcus Bussey, 'Intimate Futures: Bringing the Body into Futures Work', *European Journal of Futures Research* 53, no. 2 (2014). https://doi.org/10.1007/s40309-014-0053-6.
17. Riel Miller, *Transforming the Future: Anticipation in the 21st Century* (Paris: UNESCO and Abingdon: Routledge, 2018).
18. Can an item that has had all of its parts replaced remain fundamentally the same item? Plutarch, Theseus 75 ACE. http://classics.mit.edu/Plutarch/theseus.html; UK TV Sitcom Only Fools and Horses, 'Heroes and Villains' (1996).
19. Rebecca Coleman,. 'Things That Stay: Feminist Theory Duration and the Future', *Time and Society* 17, no. 1 (2008): 85–102. https://doi.org/10.1177/0961463X07086303.
20. Elizabeth Grosz, 'Thinking the New: Of Futures yet Unthought', in *Becomings: Explorations in Time, Memory and Futures*, edited by Elizabeth Grosz (Ithaca, NY: Cornel University Press 1999), 15–28.
21. Ernst Bloch, *The Principle of Hope* (Cambridge, MA: The MIT Press, 1959/1986).
22. Martin Heidegger, *Poetry, Language, Thought*, trans. Albert Hofstadter (New York, NY: Harper Perennial Modern Thought, 1971/2013).
23. Martin Heidegger, *Poetry, Language, Thought*, trans. Albert Hofstadter (New York, NY: Harper Perennial Modern Thought, 1971/2013).
24. Gavin J. Andrews, Mark Sudwell and Andrew C. Sparkes, 'Towards a Geography of Fitness: An Ethnographic Case Study of the Gym in British Bodybuilding Culture', *Social Science and Medicine* 60, no. 4 (2005): 877–891. http://doi.org/10.1016/j.socscimed.2004.06.029.
25. Roberta Sassatelli, 'Introduction: Bodies, Consumers and the Ethnography of Commercial Gyms', in *Fitness Culture. Consumption and Public Life* (London: Palgrave Macmillan, 2010), 1–16.
26. Mark Greif, 'Against Exercise', in *Against Everything: On Dishonest Times* (London: Verso, 2016), Section 1 Kindle.
27. Matthew B. Crawford, *Shop Class as Soulcraft: An Inquiry into the Value of Work* (London: Penguin, 2010).
28. Sven Lindqvist, *Bench Press* (London: Granta Books, 2003).
29. Albert Camus, *The Myth of Sisyphus and Other Essays* (New York: Alfred A. Knopf, 1955).
30. *Bible* In Exodus 30:34 English Standard Version.

31. *Bible* Psalm 141:2 English Standard Version.

32. Andrew Williams, 'Spiritual Landscapes of Pentecostal Worship, Belief, and Embodiment in a Therapeutic Community: New Critical Perspectives', *Emotion, Space and Society* 19 (2016): 45–55. https://doi.org/10.1016/j.emospa.2015.12.001.

33. Julian Holloway, 'The Space That Faith Makes: Towards a (Hopeful) Ethos of Engagement', in *Religion and Place: Landscape, Politics and Piety*, edited by Peter Hopkins, Lily Kong and Elizabeth Olson (Dordrecht: Springer, 2013), 203–218.

34. Kristine Krause, 'Space in Pentecostal Healing Practices Among Ghanaian Migrants in London', *Medical Anthropology* 33, no. 1 (2014): 37–51. https://doi.org/10.1080/01459740.2013.846339; Birgit Meyer, 'Mediation and Immediacy: Sensational Forms, Semiotic Ideologies and the Question of the Medium', *Social Anthropology* 19, no. 1 (2011): 23–39. https://doi.org/10.1111/j.1469-8676.2010.00137.x; Bruno Reinhardt, 'Soaking in Tapes: The Haptic Voice of Global Pentecostal Pedagogy in Ghana', *Journal of the Royal Anthropological Institute* 20, no. 2 (2014): 315–336. https://doi.org/10.1111/1467-9655.12106.

35. Mark Wynn, 'Renewing the Senses: Conversion Experience and the Phenomenology of the Spiritual Life', *International Journal for Philosophy of Religion* 72 (2012): 211–226. https://doi.org/10.1007/s11153-011-9293-6.

36. Birgit Meyer, 'Religious Sensations. Why Media, Aesthetics and Power Matter in the Study of Contemporary Religion', Inaugural Address. Amsterdam: Vrije University, 2006. http://dare.ubvu.vu.nl/handle/1871/10311.

37. Allison Hayes-Conroy and Jessica Hayes-Conroy, 'Visceral Geographies: Mattering, Relating, Defying Boundaries', *Geography Compass* 4, no. 9 (2010): 1273–1283. https://doi.org/10.1111/j.1749-8198.2010.00373.x.

38. Allison Hayes-Conroy and Jessica Hayes-Conroy, 'Visceral Geographies: Mattering, Relating, Defying Boundaries', *Geography Compass* 4, no. 9 (2010): 1273–1283. https://doi.org/10.1111/j.1749-8198.2010.00373.x.

39. David Crouch, 'Spacing, Performing and Becoming: Tangles in the Mundane', *Environment and Planning A: Economy and Space* 35, no. 11 (2003): 1945–1960. https://doi.org/10.1068/a3585.

40. Allison Hayes-Conroy and Jessica Hayes-Conroy, 'Visceral Geographies: Mattering, Relating, Defying Boundaries', *Geography Compass* 4, no. 9 (2010): 1273–1283. https://doi.org/10.1111/j.1749-8198.2010.00373.x.

41. David Crouch and Colin Ward, *The Allotment: Its Landscape and Culture* (Nottingham: Five Leaves Publications, 1988/1997).

42. Rebecca Sandover, 'Experiential Learning and the Visceral Practice of "Healthy Eating"', *Geography* 100, no. 3 (2015): 152–158.

43. Ya-hui Su, 'Lifelong Learning as Being: The Heideggerian Perspective', *Adult Education Quarterly* 61, no. 1 (2010): 57–72. https://doi.org/10.1177/0741713610380442.

44. Martin Heidegger, *Poetry, Language, Thought*, trans. Albert Hofstadter (New York, NY: Harper Perennial Modern Thought, 1971/2013).

45. Anderson Blanton, 'Sensing the Unseen: The Materiality of Prayer', *The Materiality of Prayer, The Prayer Blog. Reverberations: New Directions in the Study of Prayer*, accessed 19 May 2020. http://forums.ssrc.org/ndsp/2013/05/02/sensing-the-unseen/.

46. John-David Dewsbury and Paul Cloke, 'Spiritual Landscapes: Existence, Performance and Immanence', *Social & Cultural Geography* 10, no. 6 (2009): 695–711. https://doi.org/10.1080/14649360903068118.

47. Rosi Braidotti, *Metamorphoses: Towards a Materialist Theory of Becoming* (Cambridge: Polity Press, 2001).

48. Elizabeth Grosz, *Time Travels: Feminism, Nature, Power* (Durham and London: Duke University Press, 2005).

49. Erving Goffman, *Behaviour in Public Places: Notes on the Social Organization of Gatherings* (New York: The Free Press, 1963); Erving Goffman, *Stigma: Notes on the Management of Spoiled Identity* (Englewood Cliffs, NJ: Prentice-Hall, 1963).

50. Ernst Bloch, *The Principle of Hope* (Cambridge, MA: The MIT Press, 1959/1986), 149.

51. Martin Heidegger, 'The Question Concerning Technology', in *Basic Writings*, trans. David Farrell Krell (London: Routledge, 2011), 213–238.

Works Cited

Adam, Barbara. *Time* (Cambridge, UK: Polity, 2004).

Andrews, Gavin J., Mark Sudwell and Andrew C. Sparkes. 'Towards a Geography of Fitness: An Ethnographic Case Study of the Gym in British

Bodybuilding Culture', *Social Science and Medicine* 60, no. 4 (2005): 877–891. http://doi.org/10.1016/j.socscimed.2004.06.029.

Bergson, Henri. *Key Writings*, ed. Keith Ansell Pearson and John O'Maoilearca. (London: Bloomsbury, 2014).

Blanton, Anderson. 'Sensing the Unseen: The Materiality of Prayer', *The Materiality of Prayer, The Prayer Blog. Reverberations: New Directions in the Study of Prayer*, Accessed May 19, 2020. http://forums.ssrc.org/ndsp/2013/05/02/sensing-the-unseen/.

Bloch, Ernst. *The Principle of Hope* (Cambridge, MA: The MIT Press, 1959/1986).

Braidotti, Rosi. *Metamorphoses: Towards a Materialist Theory of Becoming* (Cambridge: Polity Press, 2001).

Bussey, Marcus. 'Intimate Futures: Bringing the Body into Futures Work', *European Journal of Futures Research* 53, no. 2 (2014). https://doi.org/10.1007/s40309-014-0053-6.

Camus, Albert. *The Myth of Sisyphus and Other Essays* (New York: Alfred A. Knopf, 1955).

Coleman, Rebecca. 'Things That Stay: Feminist Theory Duration and the Future', *Time and Society* 17, no. 1 (2008): 85–102. https://doi.org/10.1177/0961463X07086303.

Crawford, Matthew. B. *Shop Class as Soulcraft: An Inquiry into the Value of Work* (London: Penguin, 2010).

Crouch, David. 'Spacing, Performing and Becoming: Tangles in the Mundane', *Environment and Planning A: Economy and Space* 35, no. 11 (2003): 1945–1960. https://doi.org/10.1068/a3585.

Crouch, David and Colin Ward. *The Allotment: Its Landscape and Culture* (Nottingham: Five Leaves Publications, 1988/1997).

de Jouvenel, Bertrand. *The Art of Conjecture*, trans. Nikita Lary (New Brunswick: Transaction Publishers, 2012).

Deleuze, Gilles and Felix Guattari. *A Thousand Plateaus: Capitalism and Schizophrenia*, trans. Brian Massumi (Minneapolis, MN, University of Minnesota Press, 1987).

Derrida, Jaques. *Speech and Phenomena: And Other Essays on Husserl's Theory of Signs*, trans. David B. Allison (Evanston: Northwestern University, 1967/1973).

Dewsbury, John David and Paul Cloke. 'Spiritual Landscapes: Existence, Performance and Immanence', *Social & Cultural Geography* 10, no. 6 (2009): 695–711. https://doi.org/10.1080/14649360903068118.

Elias, Norbert. *What Is Sociology?*, trans. Stephen Mennell and Grace Morrisey (New York: Columbia University Press, 1984).

Engen, Trygg. *The Perception of Odors* (New York: Academic Press, 1982).

Goffman, Erving. *Behaviour in Public Places: Notes on the Social Organization of Gatherings* (New York: The Free Press, 1963).

Goffman, Erving. *Stigma: Notes on the Management of Spoiled Identity* (Englewood Cliffs, NJ: Prentice-Hall, 1963).

Goffman, Erving. *Interaction Ritual: Essays on Face-to-Face Behaviour* (New York: Anchor Books, 1967).

Greif, Mark. 'Against Exercise', in *Against Everything: On Dishonest Times* (London: Verso, 2016), Section 1 Kindle.

Grosz, Elizabeth. 'Thinking the New: Of Futures yet Unthought', in *Becomings: Explorations in Time, Memory and Futures*, edited by Elizabeth Grosz (Ithaca, NY: Cornell University Press, 1999), 15–28.

Grosz, Elizabeth. *Time Travels: Feminism, Nature, Power* (Durham and London: Duke University Press, 2005).

Hayes-Conroy, Allison and Jessica Hayes-Conroy, 'Taking Back Taste: Feminism, Food and Visceral Politics', *Gender, Place and Culture* 15, no. 5 (2008): 461–473. https://doi.org/10.1080/09663690802300803.

Hayes-Conroy, Allison and Jessica Hayes-Conroy, 'Visceral Geographies: Mattering, Relating, Defying Boundaries', *Geography Compass* 4, no. 9 (2010): 1273–1283. https://doi.org/10.1111/j.1749-8198.2010.00373.x.

Hegel, Georg Wilhelm Friedrich. *Phenomenology of Spirit* (Oxford: Oxford University Press, 1978).

Heidegger, Martin. *Being and Time*, trans. Joan Stambaugh (Albany, NY: State University of New York Press, 1953/2010).

Heidegger, Martin. 'The Question Concerning Technology', in *Basic Writings*, trans. David Farrell Krell (London: Routledge, 2011), 213–238.

Heidegger, Martin. *Poetry, Language, Thought*, trans. Albert Hofstadter. New York, NY: Harper Perennial Modern Thought, 1971/2013.

Heraclitus. *Fragments*, trans. Brooks Haxton (London: Penguin Classics, 500 BCE/2003).

Herz, Rachel S. 'The Role of Odor-Evoked Memory on Psychological and Physiological Health', *Brain Science* 6, no. 3 (2016): 22. https://doi.org/10.3390/brainsci6030022.

Holloway, Julian. 'The Space That Faith Makes: Towards a (Hopeful) Ethos of Engagement', in *Religion and Place: Landscape, Politics and Piety*, edited by Peter Hopkins, Lily Kong, Elizabeth Olson (Dordrecht: Springer, 2013), 203–218.

Husserl, Edmund. *On the Phenomenology of the Consciousness of Internal Time (1983–1917)*, trans. John Barnett Brough (Dordrecht: Kluwer Academic Publishers, 1991).

Krause, Kristine. 'Space in Pentecostal Healing Practices Among Ghanaian Migrants in London', *Medical Anthropology* 33, no. 1 (2014): 37–51. https://doi.org/10.1080/01459740.2013.846339.

Lindqvist, Sven. *Bench Press* (London: Granta Books, 2003).

Meyer, Birgit. 'Mediation and Immediacy: Sensational Forms, Semiotic Ideologies and the Question of the Medium', *Social Anthropology* 19, no. 1 (2011): 23–39. https://doi.org/10.1111/j.1469-8676.2010.00137.x.

Meyer, Birgit. 'Religious Sensations. Why Media, Aesthetics and Power Matter in the Study of Contemporary Religion', Inaugural Address. Amsterdam: Vrije University, 2006. http://dare.ubvu.vu.nl/handle/1871/10311.

Miller, Riel. *Transforming the Future: Anticipation in the 21st Century* (Paris: UNESCO and Abingdon: Routledge, 2018).

Proust, Marcel. *In Search of Lost Time: The Way by Swann's Vol. 1*, trans. Lydia Davis (London: Penguin Classics, 2003).

Reinhardt, Bruno. 'Soaking in Tapes: The Haptic Voice of Global Pentecostal Pedagogy in Ghana', *Journal of the Royal Anthropological Institute* 20, no. 2 (2014): 315–336. https://doi.org/10.1111/1467-9655.12106.

Richardson, John. *Heidegger* (London: Routledge, 2012).

Sandover, Rebecca. 'Experiential Learning and the Visceral Practice of 'Healthy Eating', *Geography* 100, no. 3 (2015): 152–158.

Sassatelli, Roberta. 'Introduction: Bodies, Consumers and the Ethnography of Commercial Gyms', in *Fitness Culture. Consumption and Public Life* (London: Palgrave Macmillan, 2010), 1–16.

St Augustine. *Confessions*, trans. Henry Chadwick (Oxford: Oxford University Press, 2008).

Su, Ya-hui. 'Lifelong Learning as Being: The Heideggerian Perspective', *Adult Education Quarterly* 61, no. 1 (2010): 57–72 https://doi.org/10.1177/074 1713610380442.

Willander, Johann and Maria Larsson, 'Olfaction and Emotion: The Case of Autobiographical Memory', *Memory Cognition* 35, no. 7 (2007): 1659–1663. https://doi.org/10.3758/BF03193499.

Williams, Andrew. 'Spiritual Landscapes of Pentecostal Worship, Belief, and Embodiment in a Therapeutic Community: New Critical Perspectives', *Emotion, Space and Society* 19 (2016): 45–55. https://doi.org/10.1016/j.emo spa.2015.12.001.

Wynn, Mark. 'Renewing the Senses: Conversion Experience and the Phenomenology of the Spiritual Life', *International Journal for Philosophy of Religion* 72 (2012): 211–226. https://doi.org/10.1007/s11153-011-9293-6.

17

Snidge

Kerry Hadley-Pryce

For some people (academics, mostly), the Black Country is an 'imagined community' which exists only in the minds of residents of the four Metropolitan Boroughs of Dudley, Sandwell, Walsall and Wolverhampton. For others, the Black Country is an ugly, grimy, industrial hinterland, often inaccurately regarded as a run-down 'part of Birmingham', a place where people talk as if black smoke is all there is to breathe. To describe the Black Country as 'grim' though is wrong, and tiresome. There is absolutely nothing grim about it.

Listen:

Brierley Hill
Cradley Heath
Pensnett Chase
Brockmoor
Buckpool

K. Hadley-Pryce (✉)
University of Wolverhampton, Wolverhampton, UK

S. Groes et al. (eds.), *Smell, Memory, and Literature in the Black Country*,
https://doi.org/10.1007/978-3-030-57212-9_17

Woodside
Gornal Wood
Primrose Hill
Hawbush
High Oak
Tansey Green
Coopers Bank
Round Oak
Bumble Hole
Wrens Nest

Place names, these are. Black Country place names. There are plenty more. You wouldn't think that place names like this would be part of something *ugly*, would you? These are historic names, pastoral in quality, a bit like poetry, a bit beautiful, really. Arty, almost. If you look at the landscape, there are housing estates high up, on hills, as if spilling out of volcanos. Perhaps that's what this place is: something waiting to erupt. Looking at it, it seems as if it could have been here before any of us, before anything at all, in fact. You can see the layers of it, even from a distance—especially so—if you care to look for it. And you should—look for it. See, the Black Country is more than just a post-industrial sprawl, lined with canals and flush with shopping centres. It's more than just a liminal zone that defies maps. It certainly is *not* a suburb of Brum.

To experience the Black Country is to experience an edgeland within an edgeland. There are extra-urban spaces, and wildspaces and wildernesses. Go and have a walk under the viaduct in Lye and out towards the river if you want to see how quickly you can morph from the urban to the rural. You'll be able to smell that lowish hum of rapeseed, ammonia and diesel, old rain and charcoal there. All of which makes you cognisant of a very particular interplay between the urban and the rural—both press against each other, just to confuse you, or enthuse you, or both. Look closely, see the hidden working farms just the other side of Stourbridge, and up Gornal way. There are lines of footfall alongside dry-stone walls and hawthorn hedges there. Not proper paths. They call them desire paths: lines made by walking. And yes, there are factories, of course, and the sudden juxtapositioning of claustrophobic urban space next to open fringes of land, which makes any definition or location of a border or threshold of the place a bit blurred. But watching, for example, a Black Country sunset can actually be like watching something emerging out of your deepest, *deepest* imagination. The Black Country sky is big. Huge. Blink and it can just stop being stone grey and can suddenly be the very beginnings of the reddest streaks and torn ribbons of spectacular silver emptied-out cloud before it pinks out into that ambiguous zone that is just-before-night. It's quick, that transition, as if time is of the essence. You have to see it to believe it.

You might think there are peculiar patches of greenery, and sometimes there is a pony, or a goat, or both, tethered on a corner. This is normal. Children still learn to ride horses—and will do, through the streets of Pensnett—bare-back, and no-one bats an eye. And the Fens Pools simmer like lochs, like an oasis, in a patch in the middle of strings of local authority housing on an undulating path, seemingly into infinity. It's a mini-wilderness. And even though some of those houses and flats there are like bomb-shelters in design, at night the lights of Lye town and Pensnett and Stourbridge and Merry Hill and Dudley shimmer in dips and ridges, and there's something enchanting about that.

Understand that the Black Country is not of the now. Its sense of time is its own. And though there is this mix of old and new, of history and new development, of urban and rural, yes, but there is also something of the future, and that might appear a complicated mistake of urban planning or simply strangely out of focus, on the contrary, everything is linked and clear, everything nudges against everything. There is no threat, instead, there is a particular cohesion—even between the now-unused and still-unused spaces, and between communities there. You might, from the outside, think of the Black Country as having an otherness that is unusual or uncomfortable: the cadence of the accent, the abbreviated words of the dialect, you might hear a certain menace in that. You might inhale and catch a breath of Tipton as warm, wet metal. You might sense the casting of iron. You might hear the furnace flames and feel the sensation of the honeyed smoke and the sweat of glass making. Imagine that now as a cone of heat, a funnel-shaped thing, sitting close to a horizon where trees stand like shambling academics.

Which surely is enough to fire up anyone's imagination.

18

Conclusion: The Futures of the Black Country—A Manifesto

R. M. Francis and Sebastian Groes

Black Country Poetics

The Black Country has become the source and subject of an increasingly intense and almost feral imaginative energy in the twenty-first century, when Britain continues to attempt to overcome its post-imperial trauma, the decline of its status as world leader on the global political stage, the growing divide between rich and poor, and decreasing support for cultural projects. With the help of writers, artists and other creatives, this weird and eerie part of the world is reimagining itself in the light of a post-industrial status that seemed to leave them behind. Black Country writing, according to McDonald, has 'a marked ambivalence toward the region itself: typically it presents a conflict between the rural and industrial, with the former seen as a benign antidote to the latter' (p. xx). Their writing has persistently voiced concern about the fact that the region has been—ever since the closing of industry in

R. M. Francis (✉) · S. Groes
University of Wolverhampton, Wolverhampton, UK

the 1970s and 1980s—neglected and forgotten. In a sense, many writers show a curious paradoxical position whereby they both looked to the past nostalgically, but also complained about the lack of change and transformation that the region experienced. Their collective goal has been to voice their concerns together: to resist neglect, to celebrate this strange place, and to place the Black Country on the (literary) map. Together they have already written what Anthony Cartwright called The Great Wolverhampton Novel.

Brexit was an important, catalysing process for the population, which overwhelmingly voted in favour, not so much out of explicitly despising the European Union or racism, but because they felt they were themselves treated as second-class citizens in their own country. Cartwright's novella, *The Cut*, exemplifies this, as do his earlier works (*Afterglow*, *Heartlands*, *How I Killed Margaret Thatcher*); all of which offer nuanced criticism of the situations faced by these communities. In his post-referendum piece in Granta Magazine he references the ruins of Dudley-based Cobb's Engine House, stating, 'Anyone trying to understand what has happened to England, what happened on 23 June's referendum, and in the many years before, might do well to visit the silent engine house ruin in its green field with black crows, and ponder'. Going on to suggest, 'There's a sense, I think, that what that X in the box translates as is seventeen and a half million voices that say, we're still here'.[1]

Now, the Black Country seems to be on the brink of a wave of investment and gentrification that might help push the region from its post-industrial slumber into a more reinvigorated and prosperous future—though the Covid-19 crisis is threatening to halt that process of transformation. McDonald argues that contemporary Black Country literature does not subscribe to narratives about gentrification of the region: 'any 'resurgence', or attempts to de-stigmatise the region, are not reflected in the region's literary fiction: the negative view that informs industrial writing persists in the fiction of the deindustrialised Black Country.'

But transformation is key, especially for writers. Recent fiction is able to pinpoint more illuminating images that allow the contemporary Black Country *Zeitgeist* to shine through. One may think of the presence of fire in Cartwright's *The Cut*, for instance, where a young woman runs burning down the streets. This image recalls the long history of fire during the industrial area, as is linked to, as McDonald reminds us, of the furnaces used by chain-makers and the glass-maker's oven. He states that 'the Black Country signifies negatively: the term itself suggests a tainted region, conjuring images of a blackened country and corrupted nature'. It has been—blackened by its own 'dark satanic mills'. Yet, fire is the age-old symbol of life, creation but also of alchemy—turning base metals into gold. Fire is the symbol of destruction and consumption, but also of desire and love. Fire links with remarks made in our Introduction, and discussions about the region's Saxon heritage; Weiland the Smithy being both Blacksmith, mystic and trickster. In Black Country fiction, fire acts as a structuring image that yokes the different writerly fantasies together.

Next to fire, we have the murky, stinky waters of the cut, the maze of canals that slices up the Black Country. It is a permanent wound, the traces of a psychopathic slasher killer that was the Victorian age enacted on the landscape. Liz Berry offers an interesting take on this metaphor in her poem *Black Delph Bride,* a sort of folk horror murder ballad set on the canals of Brierley Hill. Berry writes: 'I waz the cut / lovered atween the groanin locks'.[2] Together, the classic metaphors of fire and water forge the (textual) landscape into a complex struggle between opposites that vie for domination. They are, like Romantic and Gothic traditions, preoccupied with clashes and connections between urban and rural, wild and manmade, primal and alien.

What is remarkable has been the formation of an extraordinary and loosely connected body of work by writers who have unconditionally committed their lives and writing to representing the plurality of lives in the Black Country. When looking at the work of writers including Kerry Hadley-Pryce; Liz Berry; Satnam Sanghera; Anna Lawrence Pietroni, Anthony Cartwright; Narinder Dhami; R. M. Francis; Roy Macfarlane; and Wendy Crickard to name just a few writers who are capturing the Black Country in their textual endeavours. Their writing has continuously voiced concern about the plight of Black Country folk and about the ignoring of this part of the world by the government, which has contributed to the feeling that the Black Country is an abandoned and overlooked place. Consider Joel Lane's short story, 'The Lost District', which deals with trying to recapture memory and place in a town now removed from the map. In it, his protagonist says 'when I looked it up in my new A-Z, the district no longer existed'.[3]

Together, these writers capture a Black Country texture that, just as the smells and (childhood) memories that belong to the area, are quite specific. Indeed, when reading the body of work by contemporary writers interested in voicing the region, in their world we can construe a Black Country Poetics. What unites these fictions are the following characteristics:

1. Metaphors

The Black Country generates its own metaphors. This starts, as Paul McDonald has identified, with the name itself: 'Black is linked with funerals; it is the death colour. Country, meanwhile, suggests, country*side*, nature and, by extension, life. When you blacked nature you transform it; kill it. In this respect the phrase Black Country is a yoking together of opposites. [...] The words create something of a charged image, then; a poetic one. Perhaps it is because the phrase *is* such a potent one that so many writers have taken the trouble to include it in the title of their books'.[4] Implicitly McDonald identifies a distinct linguistic ambiguity at the very heart of the area, which forms Blakean contraries or Hegelian dialectics that are seeking sublation, transcendence, progression. This is also, perhaps, a regional take on Lorca's *Duende*. Lorca's *Duende*[5] is loosely translated as 'black sounds', as McFarlane points out in an interview: 'I recognise that this *duende* is in my love poems, moments of loss, the journey of Bevan, coming to terms with my adoption, identity, injustice and racism, there was a theme resonating with hymn like beauty'.[6] These black sounds are border sounds, somewhere between beauty and ugliness, between love and rage. A perfect sonic territory for the 2016 poetry collection, *Beginning with Your Last Breath (Nine Arches Press 2016)*, which deals with movement through liminal passages, through formative experiences and coming into being or re-newing. Kerry Hadley-Pryce too foregrounds an illuminating paradox: for her, there is 'an elegant, industrial quality to any Black Country childhood memory'.

We might also see, as Esther Asprey notes in her chapter, an attention to pollution and sewerage that create a scatological poetics in which excrement comes to stand in for the entire process of production and consumption that nestled itself into the psyche during the Victorian Age. Not only Dickins's *Our Mutual Friend* (1864), but especially T. S. Eliot's *The Waste Land* (1922) established the analogy between the industry, money and excrement. Sathnam Sanghera jokingly refers to the region in this way: 'Wolverhampton, the arse of the Black Country, in itself the bumrack of the West Midlands, in itself the backside of Great Britain'.[7] Liz Berry commented on this in a 2015 interview, stating: it's a 'very subversive idea in lots of ways because it's both repulsive and fascinating and delightful […] I suppose it's where the darkside of the erotic can be found, especially sensuality and women's sensuality […] people have talked about it as earthy and I think earthy is as close as they can get to saying sort of the dirt, the filth or the muck of it'.[8]

In his chapter on place identity, Francis evokes two distinct metaphors. Firstly, building on a 'quilt of memory', we can see how both individual and collective memory is fabricated into a shared, communal sense of identity. This metaphor is distinctly female: it harks back not only to the domestic activity of women making quilts, but it also goes back to the industrial era when immigrant women employed in the West Midlands' textile industry produced garments. Secondly, Francis brings back the Deleuzian rhizome metaphor—the centreless, organic growth below the surface of the soil that connects everything together. The Black Country is becoming less insular and divorced from the world. This is evident in Meera Syal's *Anita and Me* (1996). Set in the fictional Tollington, an imagined outer suburb of Wolverhampton, the characters watch the slow expanding of the urban environment, alongside the slow changes of the old industrial village and Meena's own acceptance of her British-Asian identity: 'I saw that Tollington had lost its edges and boundaries, that the motorway bled into another road and another and the Barlett estate had swallowed up the last cornfield and that my village was indistinguishable from the suburban mass that had once surrounded it and had finally swallowed it whole'.[9]

This act of conjugation is another metaphor we find in the work of Liz Berry and Anthony Cartwright. Whereas Berry remembers her mother's perfume, 'Anaïs Anaïs, white lilies over leather and wood', Cartwright remembers methyl methacrylate, a reactive resin widely used in industry—it is flammable and irritant. Note: perfume and resin are both chemically produced compounds—they signify a process of transformation and of the coming together of disparate elements. In these pages, Natalie Burdett remembers Sunday church visits drinking Irn Bru and eating crisps in the family kitchen where 'bleach mist making windows opaque' a reference and inversion of Philip Larkin's 'High Windows' (1974): the official, religious ceremonies make way for the mundane, quotidian experience while Burdett, similar to Larkin, seems to foreground quotations about the future and the uncertainty that modernity brings with it. This poetic alchemy seems pertinent in the context of Brexit and the Coronavirus too—we experience togetherness and separateness in what the media have termed 'The New Normal' in increasingly strange ways; feeling connected and alone simultaneously.

2. Materiality

As Asprey notes in Chapter 10, historically many writers pay attention to 'pollution deprivation and poverty as well as hunger and thirst' in their work. She goes on to note that '[g]iven the industrial heritage of the Black Country and the lack of any regulations concerning pollution, sewerage or working hours during the first stages of the Industrial Revolution, this is perhaps not a surprise. Much of the work we're speaking about in this book are part of and born out of culture in the Anthropocene; industry playing a particularly important part in bringing this about. This contemporary Black Country poetics is, in part, concerned with this too. A poem that does this is Roy McFarlane's 'The Beauty Scar'. Set at Sedgely Beacon, a rural space between the conurbations of Wolverhampton and Dudley, and one that sits on the site of a seventeenth-century quarry; a quintessentially Black Country space where nature re-takes the manmade. The poem describes a 'mark across the skies' and a 'blemish across the skies' and links this with the lover's scar. The poem references Elihu Burritt, the American Consul, who described the region's furnace illuminated skies as 'red by night', the poem says 'sun seeping / through a blood shot-horizon'. This is again linked to the lover's scar:

A scar that glows crimson
in the midst of our love making,
touched and kissed
a thousand times
I know its texture
ingrained across my mind
your beautiful skin next to mine.

The lover's beauty and her imperfection mirrors the beauty and imperfection of the setting. These marks or scars on the body and the landscape are boundaries; liminal spaces and experiences that mark a path for ecological awakening and learning to come to terms with one's body, race and being in the context of the post-industrial landscape. The poem finishes:

And you've learned to love it
never to hide it, on display for all to see
as if God had touched you especially
like the mark he left across the skies
over Sedgley Beacon.[10]

3. Subjectivity

Connected to this deep sense of the importance of materiality is an appreciation of the senses. Sensory perception and bodily materiality are keenly pronounced in Black Country literature—one might even say there is a heightened awareness of the ways in which the relationship between the subjective self and the external world is mediated through the senses. This subjective, sensitive self is a key driver behind many fictions, which offer themselves up as sensual psychogeographical explorations of a plurality of Black Country mindscapes. Moving back to Francis' thoughts on abjection in the area, Catherine O'Flynn offers a suitable example for this pronounced sensory detail. While many writers from and dealing with the Black Country focus on the industrial heritage or the post-industrial gloom of its landscape, Catherine O'Flynn moves in a slightly different, but no less important, direction. The borderless socio-politics and geography illustrated on the decaying estates of Anthony Cartwright's work is largely ignored by O'Flynn in exchange for the clean, sanitised world of the shopping centre. While this may not be traditional Black Country territory, the sanitised centre plays a significant role in the landscape of the Black Country, acting as a stark contrast to the conventional descriptions of forges, smoke, steel works and their ruins. It signifies the modern Black Country. For example, The Merry Hill Shopping Centre is built on the remains of the Round Oak Steelworks – a monument for the socio-political changes discussed in these works. In her novel *What Was Lost* smell features strongly as a warning sign for the crimes and hauntings of the story; 'Market Place wasn't a market place. It was a subterranean part of the shopping centre, next to the bus terminals, reserved for the non-prestige, low-end stores: fancy goods stores, cheap chemists, fake perfume sellers, stinking butchers, flammable-clothes vendors. Their smell mingled with the smell of burnt dust from the over-door heaters and made her feel sick'.[11] Mr Watkin's butcher shop, faced with almost certain commercial failure, as more and more people use the convenience of the centre, his shop turns into a haven for the abject. It becomes like a caricature of a Francis Bacon painting:

> The less meat he stocked, and the less meat he had, the less it looked like a butcher, and the more he looked like a crazy old man who collected and displayed bits of flesh in his front window [...] Thus it appeared that the chicken was taking the rabbit for a walk by its lead of sausages, over a hillock of pork under a dark red kidney sun.[12]

This humorous picture of the old butcher's shop conveys how the rise in consumer culture, symbolised by Green Oaks, is produced, almost always and almost inevitably, at the expense of local, working-class culture. O'Flynn's text suggests that the abject, and importantly its stenches, comes out of that decay.

4. History

The region's population cannot escape the weight of its industrial heritage, it acts as a significant marker for their place-identity. Likewise, these writers anchor much of their work to this: to looking back and to considering its ruins. Versions of this can be found in the important publications on Offa's Press' list: Nellie Cole's *Bella*; Emma Purshouse's *Close;* and the anthologies *The Nailmakers' Daughters* and *The Poetry of the Black Country.* And yet, as Groes points out in the introduction, there is change and hope and looking forward too. This then becomes a history that has been changing and evolving to incorporate the changing face of labour, landscape and the many different cultures, most prominently Black Caribbean and Indian, but also Polish and Romanian. Meera Syal's novel *Anita and Me* considers both of these things with wit and precision. Using Wolverhampton as her backdrop, her novel looks at cultural and family traditions, and racial and immigrant identities in the context of Britishness. This bildungsroman sets its protagonists coming-into-being in the context of the region's past too. She attends to how the borderless qualities of the region offer new, special possibilities for BAME identities. In this text we're on the edgelands of the city, the green-grey space typical of the post-industrial. Here, the protagonist explores her complicated relationships with white-working-class childhood, and Punjabi middle-class maturity. Syal explores this through various rebel-without-a-cause depictions and with her celebrated humour. Meena confesses about her father's singing; 'The songs made me realise that their was a corner of me that would be forever not England'.[13] Meena finds her identity split: she cannot fully engage with her Punjabi heritage because she lacks the language skills and cultural capital. As well as this, her naivety about her migrant status separates her from both communities. She is a 'freak of some kind, too mouthy, clumsy and scabby to be a real Indian girl, too Indian to be a real Tollington wench, but living in the grey area between all categories felt increasingly like home'.[14] And so, with chance encounters with gypsies, her adventures with the vulgar-tongued and promiscuous Anita, and her developing sense of familial duty, she represents the way BAME communities 'make room' for themselves. A case is made in this text that marginal, overlooked spaces that are reaching out in hope, make good homes for this sort of transformation.

5. Memory

Connected to the overwhelming traces of history visible everywhere in the Black Country is an importance of individual and collective memory;

Bryson's memory patchwork, discussed in Chapter 13. R. M. Francis'
Bella deals with this. With her refrain 'memory is difficult' weaving
throughout the novel, the ghost that centres the story and the story-
world, is a shared memory, passed down through generations, locked in
the post-industrial realm of Saltwells. Part of Bella's haunting pull is the
grounds that home her: a disused claypit now flourishing with flora and
fauna, where the Pensnett Railway used to run and where huge fossils
were pulled from the earth. Bella's spirit and her story, along with the
land, are the solid connecting tissues of communal memory. However,
each character in this multi perspective novel has a slightly different
version to recount, a slightly different reaction to her presence. We see
this is McFarlane's work too. 'Patterson's House' is a poem set in the
aforementioned threshold or confluence. It tells the story of 'the old man
of the neighbourhood', a guide for the teenage boys of the estate. Here
they learn about sex, anger, puberty; those emotional and physical issues
teenagers struggle with. Patterson also teaches them of 'how he lied about
his age to join the Air Force', how he was involved in the 'dawn of revolutions' and on 'meeting Malcolm X on Marshall Street'. In these 'rooms
filled with stories' the teenagers, on the cusp of adulthood, are provided
with lessons on politics, morality, social responsibility. McFarlane uses
the word 'lighthouse' and the phrase 'The light never went out'[15] arguing
that the light in the dark is a space for learning, for pride, for culture and
for becoming adult. The lights here are the memory tools that allow us to
navigate our futures. One could say this enhanced presence of memory
work surrounding the industrial past is a historical trauma, that to a large
extent is still a creative force behind Black Country writing and culture
more generally. However, we need to understand that memory is not
about looking back: memory is a tool that humans developed to plot and
plan the future. As Hawthorne's poem states; 'I realised that the ritual /
after all these years / had been passed on / from him / to me'.

6. Black Country Temporalities

This consciousness about the interrelation between history and
memory leads to an interest in exploring temporal complexities. As
Francis' *Bella* notes, 'Time is difficult'—especially in the Black Country.
Time in Black Country Poetics is complicated by the paradoxes of light

and dark, past and present, natural and manmade, ruined and reno-vated. Here, you are looking forward *and* back, facing the landscape and culture with love *and* trepidation. In the hands of Black Country poets, like Hawthorne, Purshouse, Berry and Kohli, the tiny detail of a fleeting moment becomes the sublime instance, full of the awestruck infinite and infinitesimal, dug out from layers in personal, communal and cultural histories. They act like the geologists that drew up Dudley Dud's mining plans. Kohli's 'Goldthorn Park via Dudley Road' is both a rich, long, drawn out feast and a simple short bus ride of smell memories. Wendy Crickard's whiff of 'Woodbines and Old Spice' act as a time machine, taking her back to childhood and 'spinning out of this world'. But then of a 'slowing' father. Cartwright's *How I killed Margaret Thatcher* and O'Flynn's *What Was Lost* do similar things with time and memory too. Each one has child-self and adult-self confessing, justifying, discussing with each other. In the Black Country Sublime, time talks back to itself and to its future potentialities.

7. Spatial Poetics

Not only does the Black Country Poetics establish a specific temporal complexity in writing, but it connects this temporarility to a spatial poli-tics. Indeed, the composition of Black Country fiction almost always overtly meditates on how language can represent the material land-scape—and turn it textually into a landscape of the mind. This landscape is a mix of the rural and urban, of industry and nature. In Liz Berry's sensual exploration of libraries with books and woods. Hadley-Pryce sees a double spatial othering: 'an edgeland within an edgeland. There are extra-urban spaces, and wildspaces and wildernesses'. Indeed, a preoccu-pation in contemporary Black Country Literature is an exploration of the weird, eerie, threshold-type landscapes, and the ways theses settings open up subversive, transgressive and transformative possibilities—both real landscapes and ones of the mind. Particularly apposite to this is the middle chapter of Syal's novel. It is Diwali, the festival of light. In Syal's text, this is symbolic of the movement from dark to light, ignorance to knowledge, the liminal passage. It is also important that this night is a type of carnival: an event of allowable transgression. At this opportune moment, Meena escapes the family home, wanders into the fairground and follows Anita into the 'syrupy gloom' to witness 'an immense black hole [...] a huge labyrinth of other shafts [...] bottomless and unforgiving' and then over the 'perimeter of the Big House garden'. She eventually finds the statue of Ganesh, the remover of obstacles, in the garden. This episode becomes a deliberate act of transgression, on Diwali and Carnival, a movement through the abject and the liminal, to find a god of transformation. Syal's next chapter begins with Meena's new baby brother being born; Meena is no longer just a child, she is a big sister too. Soon after Nanima, the Grandmother, arrives, helping Meena come to terms with her Indian identity. This midpoint passage in the novel is a point of passing through the in-between and towards maturity and selfhood. Set in the edgeland that is being consumed by the city, and set in the imaginative realm of the limen.

8. The Black Country is a language

The region does not only *have* a specific dialect, but that its structure of feeling operates *like* a language—an ideology, a way of thinking, a certain way of life. As Esther Asprey shows in her essay, the area has a long linguistic history that runs deep. The most poignant examples are Brendan Hawthorne, whose sensory exploration includes a fine ear for local dialect that has bagged him dialect writing awards ('Goo an fetch the tundish, me lad!'), R. M. Francis, whose *Bella* is composed out of Black Country dialect, and the late Dave Reeves who masterfully played with the different accents and dialects of the region textually and in his live performances, and whose legacy lives in almost all writers who succeed him. Hadley-Pryce says that 'the Black Country has an otherness that is unusual or uncomfortable: the cadence of the accent, the abbreviated words of the dialect, you might hear a certain menace in that'. In most cases, what we find is a palimpsest, a language composed out of many layers of register and discourses, with a fine ear to local diction and voice. Hadley-Pryce points out in her listing of Black Country place names—from Pensnett Chase to Wrens Nest—that '[t]hese are historic names, pastoral in quality, a bit like poetry, a bit beautiful, really'. Black Country language is heteroglot and complexly stratified.

9. Keep it unreal

Realism and authenticity are concepts that one might after first sight associate with the region. It's working-class heritage that is often conflated with a rough and ready realism and a down and dirty authenticity in the sixties' works of, for instance, Alan Sillitoe and, earlier, George Orwell. Yet, when looking beyond the surface of fictions such as Hadley-Pryce, Anna Lawrence Pietroni and Cartwright we can see that most fictions are interested not primarily in mapping a culture as a whole, but that we're almost always confronted with a wider mapping of Black Country culture via first person perspectives. Much like the spacial qualities, when it comes to Black Country writing, we can put authenticity and realism only in quotation marks—or, rather—question marks. In 'Slow Burn' Joel Lane wrote of an unfathomable being living in the caves of Wren's Nest. Built-in parts from the ancient rock, the industry, and the menacing teens that inhabit the Dudley estates—he wasn't completely making it up.

10. Laughter

A final characteristic of Black Country Poetics is laughter. As Asprey notes, 'humour is used across the ages to blot out the memories of having to eat poor and unpalatable food'. Indeed, Black Country culture and writing are deeply aware of the ways in which humour and irony are able to protect oneself and others against the harshness of existence during the industrial age. It is this dialogic Bakhtinian laughter that evades the singular, one-dimensional thinking and homogenising attitude that is what Mila Kundera associated with the termites of destruction—the capitalist forces of commodification and the reductionist vision of the technocratic leaders that are, at this time, once again growing in presence and power.

Black Country Futures

Where to from here? Asprey notes: 'Continuing descriptions of unemployment, loss of self-esteem, poor self-image in the eyes of the UK and
a loss of green space and physical beauty in the region abound'. The
double whammy of economic malaise of Brexit and the Covid-19 crisis
may scupper the changes of the Black Country to reassert itself.

Let's look to Stuart Connor's radical chapter that refuses to submit
itself to the insular, inward looking visions and stereotypes that we expect
from regular assertion of the Black Country. Connor evokes a new,
open and plural vision that rejects a very conscious bias of politico-
economic forces that have created a sinister logic of dominance from
which there seems no escape. This creates a defeatist attitude relying on
a poisonous self-fulfilling prophesy. Connor rejects this, and so should
we: 'Rather than a totalising force, the shared worlds of the Black
Country provide the resources and basis upon which new pathways and
futures can be shaped. These are explorations and accounts of doing,
being and becoming'. Connor evokes and develops the Black Country
in posthumanist terms thereby reminding us that beneath the ostensibly
industrial material conditions that seem to continue to determine the
Black Country's psyche and fate, this region too is now facing a twenty-
first-century future that will mean radical shifts on two levels. Firstly, we
appear to have left behind the humanist ideological pillars that in many
cases were the vehicle and perpetuation of privilege of a certain group at
the expense of large groups of marginalised minorities. If we realise this,
we may revision narratives about the contribution that centuries without
needing to reject stories about pride in place, local history and identity.
This vision is inclusive, and could lead to the realisation among regional
inhabitants that the Midlands is just as open, multicultural and diverse
as the British capital. See Narinder Dhami's brief historical account of
Indians arriving in the aftermath of the Second World War, and the
ironical change in consumption of tea, a poignant metaphor, where Starbucks is selling 'chai' while immigrant are using ordinary old teabags.

Secondly, this erosion of former privilege is reinforced by a more materialist posthumanism in which the human subject is spliced with new forms of technology that pose new questions about how to define 'the human'. Connor states: 'The past, is no longer a discretely bounded earlier time, but revealed with future temporalities in "new" ways. In this way, futures are not completely distinct from the past, but still offer a site where existing struggles, tensions and repressions can be overcome.[16] In these practices, the senses play a vital role guiding physical activity and opening up experiences and ways of being that although not known in advance, are anticipated'. In such descriptions, we can hear not only the posthuman complexities that allow us to anticipate and steer safely into a future compounded by many contingencies, but it is also the Bakhtinian laughter of Black Country writing: this laughter evades and negates any unitary or monologic language or ideology, which it destroys by asserting a dialogue and heterogeneity.

McDonald notes that: 'for the contemporary Black Country writers addressed here, the future still seems to be elsewhere'. This is an uncharacteristically negative conclusion that in fact reads against his own idea that most writers have 'a marked ambivalence' to the Black Country. Indeed, as this book shows, perceptions of the Black Country are changing for the better, with a more open, diverse and inclusive perspectives that promise a more hopeful future. Throughout this book we have seen examples of Connor's forwardlookingness and optimism; we have seen a spirit of newness manifest itself. Asprey writes, for instance, that Black Country 'dialect is changing but it is by no means dead, and in fact has been enriched through contact and enriched by the new experiences speakers in the modern Black Country region have had'. Francis also echoes Connor's vision, stating that 'one needs to be alert to this multitude of contradictions in one's views, in the history records and in the myths, but, to the same extent, open to timeless, immanent and imminent possibilities'. The Black Country seems to be awakening from its post-industrial slumber. Black Countryness is rising. The future is here, also.

Notes

1. Anthony Cartwright, *Black Country*, Granta Online https://granta.com/black-country/.
2. Liz Berry, *Black Delph Bride* in 'The Black Country (Chatto, 2014).
3. Joel Lane, 'The Lost District', in *The Lost District and Other Stories* (San Fransisco: Nightshade Books, 2006), 7.
4. McDonald, 8–9.
5. Federico Garcia Lorca, 'Theory and Play of the *Duende*', trans. A. S. Kline, in *Poetry in Translation* (2007) https://www.poetryintranslation.com/PITBR/Spanish/LorcaDuende.php [Accessed 01 August 2018], unpaginated.
6. Roy McFarlane, 'In The Booklight—Roy McFarlane & Beginning with Your Last Breath' (an interview with Sarah James, 2016) http://www.sarah-james.co.uk/?p=7636 [Accessed 03 May 2018], unpaginated.
7. Sathnam Sanghera, *If You Don't Know Me by Now: A Memoir of Love Secrets and Lies in Wolverhampton* (London: Viking, 2008), 51.
8. 'Brave New Reads', *Jonathan Morley Interviews Poet Liz Berry*, Published 18 August2015, WCNOnline, https://www.youtube.com/watch?v=oD3-jpcHaSE [Accessed 16 March 2020], unpaginated.
9. Meera Syal, *Anita and Me* (London: Harper Perrenial, 2004), 142.
10. McFarlane, 'The Beauty of a Scar', in *Beginning with Your Last Breath,* 51.
11. Catherine O'Flynn, *What Was Lost* (Birmingham: Tindall Street Press, 2008), 4.
12 O'Flynn, 10.
13. Syal, 112.
14. Syal, 149–150.
15. McFarlane, 'Patterson's House', in *Beginning with Your Last Breath,* 30–31.
16. E. Grosz 2000, 214.

Works Cited

Berry, Liz. *Black Delph Bride* in 'The Black Country' (Chatto, 2014).
Berry, Liz. 'Brave New Reads', *Jonathan Morley Interviews Poet Liz Berry*, Published 18 Aug 2015, WCNOnline, https://www.youtube.com/watch?v=oD3-jpcHaSE [Accessed 16 March 2020].

Cartwright, Anthony. *Black Country*, Granta Online https://granta.com/black-country/.

Lane, Joell. 'The Lost District', in *The Lost District and Other Stories* (San Fransisco: Nightshade Books, 2006).

Lorca, Federico Garcia. 'Theory and Play of the *Duende*', trans. A. S. Kline, in *Poetry in Translation* (2007) https://www.poetryintranslation.com/PITBR/Spanish/LorcaDuende.php [Accessed 01 August 2018].

McFarlane, Roy. 'In the Booklight—Roy McFarlane & Beginning with Your Last Breath' (an interview with Sarah James, 2016) http://www.sarah-james.co.uk/?p=7636 [Accessed 03 May 2018].

McFarlane, Roy. *Beginning with Your Last Breath* (Birmingham: Nine Arches Press, 2016).

O'Flynn, Catherine. *What Was Lost* (Birmingham: Tindall Street Press, 2008).

Sanghera, Sathnam. *If You Don't Know Me by Now: A Memoir of Love Secrets and Lies in Wolverhampton* (London: Viking, 2008).

Syal, Meera. *Anita and Me* (London: Harper Perrenial, 2004).

Index

Printed in the United States
By Bookmasters